To Harriet & Milt

Great friends

# MAN <u>OF</u> VISION

Wishing you the best in

sight

Bob Morrison

# MAN OF VISION

## THE STORY OF
## DR. ROBERT MORRISON

Based on interviews and research by:

Rosanne Knorr
Kevin Kremer

 U.S. PUBLISHING • OSPREY, FLORIDA

Published in the United States by U.S. Publishing, an imprint of:

S.I.S. Publishing
P.O. Box 1360
Osprey, FL 34229-1360

Library of Congress Cataloging-in-Publication Data is available upon request.

ISBN-13  978-0-9663335-5-8
ISBN-10  0-9663335-5-1

Printed in the United States of America

10 9 8 7 6 5 4 3 2 1

First Edition

# Dedicated with Gratitude

To: Perfect parents; beloved wife, Ruth;
   sweet daughter, Patty; fine son, Jim.

To: My brother Dr. Victor Morrison,
   whose thoughts stimulated my fascination with vision.

To: My brother Alan and my sister, Dr. Barbara Eller,
   who have always set examples of wholesomeness that
   I tried to follow; I've enjoyed their inspiration.

To: The truly excellent practitioners who have joined me
   in practice in Harrisburg, Pennsylvania.

To: The New York Medical College in Valhalla, New York;
   the Pennsylvania College of Optometry in Elkins Park,
   Pennsylvania; and the Pennsylvania State University College
   of Medicine in Hershey, Pennsylvania, who have granted
   me professorships to teach, allowing me to learn.

To: The patients in our practice and in the hospitals
   and clinics where I've worked who hoped I might be
   helpful, allowing me to learn.

To: The staff of aides who make daily work so
   meaningful and pleasant.

# CONTENTS

# Contents

# A Note to the Reader

This book has been inspired by real events during the extraordinary life and career of Dr. Robert Morrison. Its content is based largely on the reminisces and anecdotes of Dr. Morrison, supplemented with additional research.

For his part, Dr. Morrison made every effort to recall the facts accurately. To the best of his knowledge, they are correct; any errors are inadvertent and he apologizes for them.

As the book was being written, patient confidentiality was honored fully. Therefore, any comments regarding a particular patient's condition in this book were uncovered during research in newspapers, magazines, and other sources.

- Kevin Kremer
Editor

# MAN OF VISION

# PROLOGUE

T HEY HAD ALMOST MADE IT BACK HOME BEFORE THE LAW CAUGHT
up with them.

Robert Morrison, his wife, and his good friend Ruff had left
Harrisburg, Pennsylvania, at seven that morning so they could get
to Baltimore Harbor on time. All had gone smoothly at first. They
made good time and enjoyed the drive except for the unsettling
news on the radio about Vietnam protests across the country.

Somehow, just the mention of boys dying in Southeast Asia
and the crowds of Americans protesting it made the purpose of
this trip seem all the more superficial. Robert felt a twinge of guilt,
though he knew it was ridiculous. At 43, he was definitely too old
to be drafted. It wasn't that. It was simply that this errand represented an entirely different world and a whole lot of fun most of
the boys fighting in Vietnam would never know.

Robert shut off the radio. By the time they arrived at Baltimore Harbor, he was in a good mood once more. In the Customs
Office, he signed the paperwork the agent handed him and picked
up the keys to the car that sat just outside the office.

"That's a real conversation piece," the official commented. He
looked Robert over with a touch of envy. Quite natural, Robert

supposed, as he thought back to the state of the country these days and still felt self-conscious. The envy brought on by the extraordinary car embarrassed him. He, of all people, was about to drive out of here like a rock star in a glossy black Rolls-Royce delivered directly from a queen.

Still, he couldn't help but admire the sleek lines of the classic vehicle. He remembered the Rolls well from the first time he'd ridden in it in Amsterdam. Before they'd begun that ride, the queen's chauffeur had removed the license plates that indicated it was the queen's automobile, and he'd replaced them with other plates. Robert smiled, remembering the destination.

The chauffeur had taken Robert for a tour of Amsterdam's infamous Red Light District, referred to many times as *the girls in the windows*. The area included several blocks lined with women of all ages and descriptions, sitting on display in large windows, a tiny sink nearby, as they awaited customers.

When a customer arrived, the girl would pull a drape until business was done (which seemed to be only a few minutes). Then she'd open the drapes, sit again, awaiting the next customer. The irony didn't escape Robert—the queen's Rolls-Royce driving past the ladies of the night as they posed in picture windows.

The car was a real beauty. The black paint gleamed. The interior was a soft, rosy, red leather. The hood swooped royally. Robert's impish self returned with the thought that the car had a better lineage than he did.

As Robert stood admiring the car at Baltimore's harbor, he walked around the trunk, and another, more practical thought dawned on him. The Rolls didn't have a license plate. He'd been so involved in planning to pick the car up—getting it home without it being registered had never occurred to him. He was in Baltimore and home was Harrisburg, more than an hour's drive away.

He called over to Ruff, who was to follow them home in the Chevy. "Ruff, on the way back, just drive close behind me. Hopefully, no one will notice the missing plate."

ThEY WERE JUST TWO BLOCKS FROM HOME WHEN THE POLICE CAR pulled beside the Rolls, and the flashing lights indicated that Robert should stop.

"Are you aware, sir, that you're missing a license plate?"

The jig was up. It was now a matter of trying to avoid a ticket by explaining. The policeman *might* understand. After all, the situation was a bit unusual.

"I apologize, Officer. I just picked this car up in Baltimore and ..."

The policeman scowled. *Dang.* Now he'd done it. Robert had just admitted he'd driven this car for almost 80 miles, knowing full well he was driving illegally without a license plate. Robert tried again.

"You see, I didn't know it wouldn't have a plate—or rather, I didn't think about that part of it. And I couldn't leave the Rolls in Baltimore Harbor. It's a special gift," he added lamely.

"Yeah, nice friends to give you a Rolls-Royce." The voice held more than a touch of sarcasm. Robert imagined the policeman processing a series of thoughts which might just have involved drugs or alcohol—or white slavery, for all he knew.

Ruthie had been sitting quietly next to him, but now she piped up. "Officer, my husband really didn't know this would be a problem. We're very sorry but we live near here and we had to get the car home. Queen Juliana of the Netherlands gave it to him." Ruthie said this with the same matter-of-fact pride she used when she told their friends how good Robert was about helping around the house.

The policeman paused for a split second to process this new piece of information. The sarcasm was thicker now. "You know, fella. I've heard a lot of fairy tales, but this takes the cake. Your driver's license, please."

"Officer, I know it's hard to believe—"

"You've got that right. If this car came from the Queen of the Netherlands, I'm one of the Beatles."

Robert touched the lustrous wood of the glove box and pulled out the paperwork he'd received at the Customs Office. He handed it to the policeman. At least it would prove the car's origins.

The officer scanned it. He traced the royal seal with his finger and felt the embossed surface with the tip of his thumb. He looked at Robert. He looked back at the piece of paper in his hand.

"Queen Juliana, huh?"

The policeman looked over the trim man behind the wheel of the Rolls-Royce, who appeared confident, but not overly so, about as far from royalty as anyone could be. Yet, the proof of some undeniable exception to the rule was sitting on the side of this rural Pennsylvania road.

The homes nearby were certainly not as palatial as Her Majesty's Royal Mews which the Rolls-Royce had left six weeks prior. But, as Robert explained, the automobile had been one of 17 built especially for Queen Juliana of the Netherlands and her consort, Prince Bernhard. They were giving him the car as a present.

"So it came directly from this queen's palace?" asked the policeman, now intrigued.

"It made the tour of Amsterdam's Red Light District first," Robert laughed. "Would you like to hear that story?"

Ruthie prodded his arm and whispered, "Bobby, this is not the best time to joke."

Robert smiled as if to say he really didn't care. He wasn't going to take this nearly as seriously as the rest of the world.

The policeman leaned forward. This had broken what had been an otherwise routine patrol. After all, it wasn't every day that one of their local residents showed up in a queen's Rolls-Royce. He could understand it if the recipient was the governor or other highly placed politician or something. Or perhaps a Broadway star playing at the simple life in a Pennsylvania mansion. But, no.

To add to the mystery, this man, though titled as a doctor, didn't appear to be particularly famous. Robert Morrison wasn't a renowned cardiologist like the South African, Dr. Christiaan Barnard, who had just performed the world's first heart transplant. Robert hadn't created insulin, the polio vaccine, or a cure for cancer.

He was, in simple fact, an eye doctor. And, as Dr. Robert Morrison was the first to admit, that was all he wanted to be. The fame and fortune became his through an extraordinary devotion to achievement in his field. That devotion resulted in an invention that millions of people adopted eagerly in order to improve their lives, their looks, and their health.

The policeman didn't know all that. But on that sunny day in early March, his curiosity got the best of him and he had patience. This was one story he wanted to hear.

# 1

## "I SHOULD HAVE STUDIED MORE"

MIKE DOUGLAS ONCE INTERVIEWED THE VERY ACCOMPLISHED Dr. Robert Morrison on network television and asked, "Do you have any regrets about your life, Dr. Morrison? Is there anything you'd do differently if you had it to do all over again?"

Robert answered without hesitation. "I would have studied more."

"That seems like a strange answer for a man with your achievements. You helped develop soft contact lenses. You are the eye doctor to celebrities and royal families all over the world."

Robert laughed. "When I was in school, I spent more time with the girls and social life than studying. Oh, and there was tennis. I wasn't bad for a local player. I played number one position in high school and even won some tournaments." He sounded especially proud of the last part.

"Are you simply a natural genius?"

"Hardly. I suppose you could say I was a late bloomer ... a very late bloomer. I did things backwards. I finally started studying *after* I graduated from college."

"What happened to change your mind?"

"It suddenly occurred to me that I was going to be doing this work the rest of my life. I wanted to be good—very good at what

I was doing."

Robert said this with almost religious fervor. This was a man who had decided what his mission would be in life, and nothing was going to stop him.

Robert Jay Morrison invented vision products that improved the lives of millions worldwide. He became the trusted confidant of royalty and celebrities, and he achieved fame and fortune far beyond what he or his family would ever have imagined. However, nothing about his early years, not even his university or graduate school days, hinted at the success he later achieved in his life.

Calvin Coolidge won his second term as President a month before Robert Jay Morrison's birth. His fellow students called him Jay in his early years, and he accepted it as his first name, never realizing that the birth certificate issued on December 1, 1924, in Harrisburg, Pennsylvania, had indicated Robert Jay Morrison, not Jay Robert.

Robert's parents never said a word to their four children about achieving the highest grades in school. Alan, Robert, Barbara, and Victor always wanted their mom and dad to be proud of them even if their parents never pushed them to study more or get better grades. Robert tended to focus on social activities and sports more than academics.

To say Robert was a lackadaisical student might be a bit harsh. It was clear, however, that he was more devoted to tennis and girls than he was to books. He was outgoing and sociable, among the first to attend a party or get ready for a tennis game—if it was a tennis tournament, all the better. He'd go all out to win and many times he did.

His parents expected their children to continue their education after high school, but when the time came, Robert didn't know what field he wanted to study. His broad aspiration was simply to do something in health care. Whether it would be as a family physician, a psychiatrist, dentist, orthopedist, or any of dozens of specialized fields, he hadn't a clue.

Robert began by attending Pennsylvania State University as a premed student. He didn't follow a specific course of study, just a general curriculum. As an entering student, he didn't have any idea what degree he wanted. That, in itself, did not encourage an extraordinary effort. It's difficult to be motivated to reach a goal when the goal isn't known.

He was saved having to narrow down the field by World War II. After just one year at Penn State, he asked his mother for his birth certificate to show the Army recruiters. When he had his birth certificate in hand, he noted the reverse order of his names—Robert Jay, not the Jay Robert he'd assumed—and he began going by his real first name.

He joined the Army in 1943. Like many of his fellow students and his two brothers, Robert felt a patriotic urge to serve his country. By this time, World War II had been fought for several years, and Robert's youthful patriotism surged after seeing a film on the horrors taking place in Germany and Japan. He and his brother Alan both went into the service the same day. At the time, Robert didn't realize how difficult this was for his parents. By applying together, Robert thought Alan and he would be assured of being assigned to the same base. They were—for three days. Then they were separated and sent to different locations for training, Alan to Miami and Robert to North Carolina. In Robert's case, his impetuous nature was enough to encourage him to be where the action was.

He was shot down by his captain. Robert remembered how the officer did it, with words that put him in his place as the enlistee who had very little power over his own fate.

"No one in battle is there because they decided to be there. The Army will train you. The Army will decide where you'll go. So, Morrison, take a cold shower and lighten up."

To Robert's chagrin, the Army decided he'd serve in various camps and hospitals in the United States. Considering his quiet and peaceful demeanor, performing various medical duties was probably the best thing for him to do. Despite his personal disappointment at not serving overseas, he served and was later honorably discharged.

He returned to his studies, this time with more enthusiasm and a solid direction. The GI Bill's benefits would pay for four years of education. It was that benefit, and the resulting time limitation, that helped shape his choice of careers.

Robert wanted to work in the health care field, but he still had no precise idea of what form that vocation would take. The field was narrowed only by the fact that he did not want to burden his middle class parents with any more expenses. The GI Bill of Rights would provide four years of education. No more.

For that reason, he reviewed careers that could be completed in just four years. Though he considered being a medical doctor, it required more premed studies before he could even apply to a professional school, and he wondered if he'd even be accepted. Besides, that would bump up the amount of time required beyond the government's financial aid.

The answer came from his younger brother, Vic, who had managed to snag a summer job in an optometrist's office. When Vic described the work involved in eye care and optics, it sounded fascinating.

So Robert applied to the Pennsylvania College of Optometry in Philadelphia, one of the professional schools that was allowing some World War II veterans entrance without the usual four years of professional schooling. This would allow Robert to complete his study in the alloted four years. At last he knew what his career would be.

His class at the Pennsylvania College of Optometry consisted largely of other veterans like himself. They were, as Robert said with some pride or rebellion, "in no mood to follow a lot of petty discipline and there was even a fair amount of cheating." His responsible self added, "Despite that, the education was good."

Once he'd determined his course of study, Robert followed the habits he'd developed during his earlier years. Girls, tennis, and social life took precedence over studying. In tennis, he excelled. It could be added that the tennis, at least, stood him in good stead later in life when he played in celebrity tennis tournaments around the world. Sometimes he even won.

If he asked a girl for a date, even if he did plan it to avoid interfering with his classes, invariably something would alter his good intentions. He might ask a girl out for a Tuesday date, but if she said she wasn't available that night but could go out on Wednesday, he'd reply, "Great!"—never mentioning the fact that he had an exam he needed to focus on that night.

It was the same with sports. If the Phillies had a good game scheduled, and the guys asked Robert to join them, seeing the ball game always came first.

In 1948, Robert donned the cap and gown and joined fellow graduates to receive his Doctor of Optometry degree. He received no honors. His name wasn't called for a special mention. Nothing set Robert Morrison apart from the sea of new graduates. As a result of years of partying and playing tennis, the future success of Robert Morrison was still far from evident.

In his first year after graduation, something clicked. As he later reminisced for Mike Douglas on national television, Robert finally considered the fact that he would be working for the rest of his life. He thought about the fact that he hadn't been the oldest in his family. He hadn't been the youngest. He hadn't been the only girl, just one of three boys. But he wanted to stand out in some way. He wanted to be good at his chosen career.

Robert began to set up a new course of study for himself, and after that, he was to learn more than he had during all his years of college put together. After all, he had to make up for lost time. His goal gave him energy and direction, challenging his native intelligence to finally be put to good use.

He read voraciously and attended every lecture he could, many at New York Medical College. He sought out experts, studied their techniques, asked questions, and listened to their advice. He took specialized courses on weekends. He attended meetings of optometrists and ophthalmologists from all over the world.

Personal visits were important to him, but he had no car and couldn't afford to take a plane, so he took trains to New York, Chicago, Las Vegas, and the University of California at Berkeley. Over the years, when he could afford to travel further afield, he followed world experts to wherever they were speaking, attending conferences in places like Acapulco, Hawaii, and the West Indies.

He did whatever it took. Robert had decided to concentrate on his career, and finally his focus was simple and direct. He would be the best he could be.

## 2

### New Practice, New Marriage

I F A PASSERBY HAD BLINKED, HE WOULD HAVE MISSED THE small shingle outside the two-room optometrist's office. It said *Dr. Robert Morrison/Optometrist*. Most of the citizens of Harrisburg, Pennsylvania—much less anyone else in the country or the world—still hadn't noticed that a new optometrist had set up shop.

Robert's novice secretary was intent on changing that. She looked pleased with herself when she walked into the reception area that morning in 1949. "Dr. Morrison," she announced, "I think we've got one."

It was only 8 a.m. No patients sat in the waiting room, though that in itself wasn't uncommon. The new practice had not acquired many patients yet. But the diligent Yvonne Powers was working on the situation, intent on helping her new boss develop his practice.

That very morning as she was coming to work, Yvonne had taken a nearly empty bus, but she chose to sit beside one of the few other passengers, an elderly man. The man seemed to be having trouble reading his paper, holding it out away from his eyes and squinting. Yvonne proceeded to explain to her fellow rider that she worked for the best optometrist in Harrisburg, and he really should give them a call for an appointment. She handed him a business card and suggested he give the office a call. She also considered riding the bus more often. It seemed to be working better than most methods for finding new patients. After all, at that time it was considered unprofessional and unethical for optometrists to advertise their services. It didn't matter. Yvonne would be the personal ambassador for Dr. Robert Morrison's practice.

Robert appreciated his secretary's dedication. Early one day in 1949 he called her into his office to take some dictation. It was a letter that was to compensate an unnamed friend with a salary increase from $17 to $18 a week. Yvonne asked if she should make out an envelope.

"No, I'll handle that," said Robert.

Three days later Yvonne received an envelope in her mailbox at home. Inside was the letter she'd typed. Robert had given her a raise. Considering the costs of the office rent, lights, heat, and lab bills that ate into the fledging practice's profits, Robert didn't mention one fact to Yvonne: she was now making more than he was.

Eventually, including bus referrals, the new practice thrived. Robert would spend a full day at the office with patients, then spend long hours at home studying new theories and techniques—making up for the lost time he felt he'd wasted in school. He attended lectures when he could during the week, and when the weekend rolled around, he often took specialized courses. When he heard about a practitioner with a special skill or technique, he'd make a special effort to visit him.

The working lifestyle was a vastly different one than what he'd indulged in at college. For once, Robert's social life took a backseat, and that meant less dating.

Robert and his brothers were all involved in a male fraternity called Pi Tau Pi. Though the purpose of the group was ambiguous, Pi Tau Pi did at least one philanthropic project a year. Beyond that, the fraternity seemed to be almost an early form of a referral or matchmaking service in that it was a way for the group to interact, meet people, and socialize. Meeting the right woman to marry was an unspoken goal.

The group had chapters in most major cities throughout the United States. Harrisburg was the smallest city within the fraternity. Each year, the group met in a different city, in what they referred to as their annual conclave. The host city was charged with the duty of supplying dates for the fraternity members. The system could have been considered a cross between a debutante ball—since it often introduced new women to the group—and an upscale version of what is now called speed dating.

The three-day event scheduled three dates per day for the men. That way the participants would be able to meet and get to know many women in the short time they had. That year, the Pi Tau Pi event was to be held at a luxurious resort hotel called Galen Hall located near Reading, Pennsylvania. Even if the love of one's life never showed up, the participants had access to all the resort facilities to enjoy swimming, tennis, golf, and fine dining.

Since Harrisburg was the host that year, the fraternity members in the group there had to supply an adequate number of attractive and available dates. They spread the net wide, enlisting everyone they knew to find the loveliest and most charming girls.

One of the Harrisburg members had found his wife through fraternity activities, and she happened to be from Allentown, Pennsylvania. She invited three girls she knew from there to the event.

The Harrisburg fraternity assigned the sociable Robert Morrison to the enviable task of greeting girls as they arrived at the hotel. He would use his charm to tactfully explain the dating system and make sure the girls weren't offended by the procedure where several dates could be arranged in one day or one evening.

For example, the committee would set up dates each evening, but there wasn't enough time for each person attending the event to be paired with everyone. Therefore, sometimes a man and a woman would meet at the pool or tennis courts, notice that they weren't scheduled for a committee-arranged date, and decide to have an unofficial date instead, usually scheduled later that evening. Thus, it was left to Robert to tactfully explain the late-date phenomenon to the young ladies, which he did by emphasizing the social aspect.

"Please don't feel bad if you have a late date and bump into your earlier date. It's part of the fun."

The system worked and it was fun. Undoubtedly, even more fun than speed dating.

The group of young women who drove from Allentown included one lady who was eager to get to know Robert, and he was able to date her. It was her roommate, Ruth, who caught Robert's eye, however. Ruth would never have an official date with Robert during that three-day event—not even an unofficial one.

Robert was too busy driving back and forth from Reading to Dickinson College. The sociable young man of the college years had flip-flopped, and the same fervor he had once had for tennis and dating was now devoted toward his career. He'd signed up for extra credits at Dickinson College during that semester, and besides the classes, he had to see patients at his office in Harrisburg. Both responsibilities put a serious crimp in his dating opportunities at the event. But he was intrigued by Ruth Rapoport.

Three weeks later, Robert paced the living room trying to decide what to say when he called Ruth. Maybe he shouldn't have waited so long to ask her for a date, but his patient load had increased, and he'd gone to visit Professor Nupuf by train. The professor had taught him how to make an impression of the eye to fit a scleral lens. The weeks had slipped by, and now he realized that it had been too long. He wasn't sure how to explain the delay in contacting her. Anyway, it was now or never.

The rotary dial made a soft whirr as he dialed the number in Allentown.

"Hello," said a soft voice he recognized from Galen Hall.

"Hello ... Ruth? This is Robert Morrison. Remember, we met at the Pi Tau Pi event."

"Yes, I remember." The voice fell silent. She wasn't making this easier for him.

"Well, I've been busy, but I have tickets to that new show *Cat on a Hot Tin Roof* Saturday. It got splendid reviews. Would you like to go?"

The split-second pause gave him a warning that the answer would not be the one he wanted. "I can't."

He mentally kicked himself. Waiting was obviously the wrong thing to have done. Maybe she was dating someone already. In three weeks? Someone she'd met at the event perhaps. She obviously had no interest in him, though.

"I have poison ivy," she said so quietly that Robert wasn't sure he'd heard correctly.

"Excuse me?"

"I have poison ivy. I can't go out." She sounded embarrassed at the fib, Robert thought to himself. He'd heard girls say they had to wash their hair before, but poison ivy was a completely novel way to send a fellow packing. He didn't know if he'd tell Alan about this or not.

He mumbled something to Ruth that was roughly, "I'm sorry to hear that. Hope you feel better soon."

They both hung up.

Months later Ruth happened to be visiting Harrisburg with a girlfriend who had asked Ruth to keep her company when she came into town to shop at Mary Sachs' Shop, known for its shoes. The girlfriend had met Robert and knew that he'd called Ruth once. She nagged Ruth to phone him. At the very least, they'd see the handsome, young optometrist again. Maybe he even had a friend. Robert invited the two girls to dinner at the Blue Ridge Country Club where he was a member. On the drive to the club, he pointed out the scenery which was pure rural Pennsylvania, serene and thick with hardwoods. A short distance down the road, he stopped the car and pointed to a lot already staked out for a home.

"That's my lot. I want to build a bachelor home there. I saw one in the movies and it looked great. Filipino house boy and all," he joked.

Ruth later told her mother, "I met a nice guy, but he's a committed bachelor and a waste of time."

Apparently, she didn't tell Robert that because he phoned her again, and she agreed to see him. When he picked her up for dinner, they sat together on the sofa talking. He put his hand on her knee casually and asked, "What are we going to do tonight?"

"The first thing we're going to do is to get your hand off my knee," Ruth shot back.

Her response didn't discourage Robert in the slightest. Five dates later they were engaged.

Robert and Ruth were married January 29, 1956. Robert's older brother, Alan, served as best man. Since Ruth had no sisters, Robert's sister, Barbara Eller, was maid of honor. The reception for the young couple was held at the Warwick Hotel in Philadelphia, then one of the city's most fashionable locations for special occasions.

Robert's DILIGENCE IN HIS PRACTICE WAS ALREADY PAYING OFF handsomely. He had a good reputation in Harrisburg and had made the acquaintance of almost a dozen eye surgeons who were referring patients to him. In those days, the surgeons would remove the cloudy cataractous lens from the eye, but the patient would still need vision corrections, so Robert would fit them with a rigid contact lens.

His work schedule was daunting, and early on, Ruth learned her new husband had enough energy for three men. He made time for work, teaching, and Ruth. She said, "He's cursed with inordinate energy and the ability to sleep fewer than six hours a night."

The young couple had lived in a furnished apartment in the building called The River House along the Susquehanna River in Harrisburg, but it didn't take long before they planned the bachelor house as their family home. Robert commuted between his office and educational seminars, and now he was considered an expert himself, so he began accepting lecture engagements at diverse locations.

He taught Thursdays at the Pennsylvania College of Optometry in Philadelphia as an associate professor of optometry and Fridays at the New York Medical College as an assistant professor of ophthalmology. To ensure he spent as little time away from home as possible, Robert rented a helicopter that took him to Philadelphia each week, then to New York City, then back home.

At one point Robert's dauntless enthusiasm got the better of him, and he decided to actually learn how to fly the helicopter himself. At the Pennsylvania College of Optometry, he was allowed to land wherever there was room for the helicopter. One time, he even called in to "request permission to land on second."

The helicopter soon made a perfect landing on the school's baseball diamond—on second base.

NEW YORK MEDICAL COLLEGE SUGGESTED A THREE-YEAR M.D. program (Medical Doctorate program) to Robert. He would be able to attend classes there in New York City, and he'd finally have the opportunity to get his M.D. degree, something he felt he couldn't afford when he first decided to work in the health care field. The school hoped this incentive would encourage Robert to remain on the faculty.

Robert was excited about the opportunity, and he immediately decided to accept the offer despite the fact that it would mean moving to New York City for three years. He spoke to his colleagues in Harrisburg and told them to hold the fort. He would return in three years.

For once, Ruth was dead set against one of her husband's bright ideas. She wanted to remain in Harrisburg. They were comfortable in their home on the lovely wooded lot. Their son, Jim, was a young child. Ruth had support in Harrisburg, and she didn't want to live in the big city.

Calling in the big guns, Ruth asked one of Robert's closest friends to speak to him. A doctor himself, Hyman Kahn, M.D., urged Robert to reconsider his pursuit of the M.D. degree. "All you are doing is changing the letter 'O' to 'M,'" he said.

The point hit home with Robert. He realized that going for the degree wasn't so much about the initials as about the joy he felt in learning all about the human body. That he could continue to do on his own. If he desired to have the M.D. influence on his practice, some ophthalmology residents had already asked about the possibility of joining him.

Ophthalmologists added the surgical dimension to his group. Already, *The Journal of the American Optometric Association* was calling Robert Morrison's practice the largest ethical practice in the United States. (Years ago, ethical in any profession meant there was no advertising other than a small sign in front of the office. Advertising meant unethical. Today, many physicians, dentists, optometrists, and other professionals advertise, yet they may be more honest and ethical than a practitioner with a small sign in front of the establishment. The meaning has changed significantly. Robert still feels uncomfortable about advertising. His practice thrived by word of mouth and the publicity he garnered as a vision expert.)

While teaching the ophthalmology residents at New York Medical College, Robert continued to see patients in Harrisburg. Two of them were the daughters of a prominent doctor, Dr. Denison. The girls did well, and Dr. Denison invited Robert to open an office next to his, in an area known for its affluence. He told Robert that he would refer all his eye cases to him. Robert opened the office and his practice grew even larger, eventually including some of Harrisburg's most elite citizens.

The lectures in New York City were becoming popular. Where once Robert had traveled all over the country to learn from eye care experts, now vision professionals were traveling to see him. Ophthalmologists and college students from throughout the area began attending his lectures.

Soon, Robert was seeing patients in New York as well as Harrisburg. The students would watch Robert work, and after each patient left, they'd have a chance to question Robert and discuss particular eye cases.

Robert was soon so busy when he was teaching at New York Medical College and seeing patients there, that the school decided to avoid making appointments for the patients. It simply wasted the allotted time if a person didn't show up. Eventually, the medical college set a yellow legal pad on a counter and people signed in as they arrived. By the time Robert walked in the door at 8:30 a.m., the sheet would be full. He would take the patients in the order they appeared on the list, but he soon discovered that many people had arrived as early as 6 a.m. to sign up, then they'd left for breakfast and came back to see Dr. Morrison.

He tried to manage the appointments, to keep the patients moving along, but his own reputation was what failed him. The crowds were becoming so large at times that it was not uncommon for patients to wait three hours to see him. This was not how he ran his private practice in Harrisburg, and he didn't like having to ask people to wait.

Nevertheless, he loved visiting New York with its diversity, the arts, the restaurants, just the buzz on the streets. The atmosphere thrilled him every time he was there.

New York Medical College moved to Valhalla, about 40 miles from New York City. The college kept Robert on the faculty as assistant professor, and Robert finally decided to open up his own office in Manhattan. At one point he kept an apartment there. He would work from early morning to mid-evening, then he'd usually meet Ruth for dinner, where they treated themselves to a meal at any of several gourmet restaurants.

It was in those New York offices that Ruth worked for just one day. She was acting as the office receptionist late one morning when a Park Avenue matron entered the waiting area, carrying a small white poodle. She stomped toward Ruth.

"I need to see the eye doctor."

Ruth looked down at the schedule sheet. "Do you have an appointment?"

The woman gestured impatiently with a flick of her right wrist, still holding the poodle tightly to her bosom with her left arm.

"No. I just want to see the doctor."

"I'm sorry but there are people waiting with appointments. If you'll give me your name, I'll put you down for the earliest time possible."

"I don't wait for anyone," the woman shot back. She stood implacable in front of Ruth who had no idea how to handle the situation. She turned her back and entered Robert's office in tears.

"I'll handle it," Robert said. He went to the waiting room where he apologized to the others and took the woman to his examination room where he examined her quickly. She asked him to check her dog's eyes, and Robert quickly glanced at them.

"He has cataracts. Take him to the vet," he said brusquely. "Now go home. You are drunk."

The woman complained bitterly but she left. Five hours later, she returned to the office and apologized for her behavior.

As for Ruth, that day was her first and last to work at the office. After that, she devoted herself to raising their children and wondering what made her husband tick.

# 3

## RIGID CONTACT LENSES USED TO TREAT MYOPIA

W HEN ROBERT HAD COMPLETED HIS TEENAGE PA-
tient's eye exam, he noticed an amazing thing: her
vision hadn't changed since she'd been to see him the previous
year. Carolyn was nearsighted, but Robert had seen enough myopia to know that it virtually always progressed, especially in children and teenagers.

While an adult's vision might not worsen in a year, a teenager
with myopia was a different case. At fifteen, Carolyn's vision had
remained at the same level it had been when he first fitted her with
new rigid contact lenses.

Robert pulled his chair closer to his desk and reviewed Carolyn's prescription. Not only was the prescription identical to what
he had written a year before, it was identical to what it had been
two years ago when Carolyn had first come to him, complaining
that she couldn't read the football scoreboard like the other kids
could.

The fact that Carolyn's eyes hadn't changed for the worse was
a good thing, of course. But what was the reason for no change?

The thought nagged at him. Robert had seen several children

and teenagers lately with the same results. Boys and girls. Different ages. Different health levels. They were typical preteens and teenagers who, as is normal for those ages, were intensely self-conscious about their appearance. They needed vision correction to see the blackboard and read what bus was coming down the street, but instead of glasses, this group had all requested contact lenses. They didn't want to be the *four eyes* in school.

Robert had fitted each young person with what was currently available, the rigid contact lens, to correct their nearsightedness. He wondered how *their* eyes were doing.

Robert moved to the file cabinet. His secretary kept everything in proper order by last name. Robert could remember some of the children's last names and pulled those files out immediately. He rifled through paperwork and reviewed the cases, comparing how their vision had progressed.

He looked at his watch. He didn't have time to go through all the files, seeking out the other young people with names he didn't remember. He marched out to the reception area.

"Colleen, I need every file on a child or teenager with myopia that I've fitted with contact lenses."

She looked up at him and repeated his request to be sure she had it right. "Everyone with contact lenses and myopia."

"On second thought, I'll compare the others as well. Every file for a child or teenager who I examined, even if they simply had glasses."

A few days later Robert was able to review the records. There were more than he expected. The practice had grown over the last several years.

He carefully compared the student prescriptions of those wearing glasses with those he had fitted with rigid contact lenses. The ones wearing regular glasses were following the normal curve and becoming more nearsighted as they got older. Nothing new there. But by the time Robert sat back in his chair with the last file, he thought he'd discovered something no one had noticed before: in those who wore the hard contact lenses, the myopia had either progressed very slowly or had not progressed at all.

The next weekend, Robert was enjoying his habit of reading the Sunday *New York Times* front to back. He was interrupted only for the breakfast Ruth cooked them.

He sat down as Ruthie dished up some scrambled eggs. He patted her protruding stomach.

"How's little Jimmy or Patty doing in there?"

"Remember when we were dating and I told you to keep your hand off my knee?" She smiled.

"Sure do," Robert said, smiling back.

She sat down and started to butter some toast.

"Ruthie, do you remember my telling you how I noticed that children wearing rigid lenses aren't becoming more myopic? It's as though the lenses are actually retarding the myopia."

Ruth had heard enough shop talk to understand Robert's point.

"Does that mean you should start prescribing the rigid lenses more often?"

"I don't want the parents to think I'm pushing them into paying for contacts."

"But if it helps the children, you're not pushing it, just telling them." She thought for a moment. "Do the lenses have the same effect on adults?"

"I don't think so. I strongly suspect it's the young people because their eyes normally change so fast. In any case, this isn't a scientific study. I can't prove anything. It's just something I've noted."

"It is curious, though."

Robert thought for a moment. "You know, I happened to read something in the *Times* the other day. It struck a chord with me and maybe there was a reason. It said, 'Never take a good idea to your grave.' This is an idea that shouldn't be hidden."

"Bobby, you're only 33."

"I'm not intending to keel over soon. Don't worry. We still have that baby to raise!"

That afternoon Robert repeatedly recalled the phrase "Never take a good idea to your grave." He decided he couldn't let his discovery, which he was convinced was a valid theory on retarding myopia, be ignored. He began taking notes and writing his theory down.

Dr. Morrison reported the findings in a paper published in the *Optometric Weekly*. He was the first to report the possible value of using rigid contact lenses, not just to improve vision, but as an actual therapeutic device to be used to control the progression of myopia or nearsightedness. He later spoke to the American Academy of Optometry, and provided a thesis of 15 possible reasons why the rigid contacts might have a therapeutic potential.

Robert made it clear that this was simply his personal observation, one that had not been subjected to the classic control groups usually required in order to establish a valid theory. However, he did describe his findings in detail. His initial report covered a wide range of children and young adults from ages seven to 19 and reported that the need for additional minus power in the rigid contact lens had not been required by this group during the first year and a half of wear. He explained the type of lens he'd used. In his study, the children had been fitted with PMMA (polymethylmethacrylate) lenses with base curves that were flatter than the flattest ophthalmometer reading.

Dr. Morrison admitted that he didn't know why rigid contact lens use appeared to retard myopia. However, his 15 theories were laid out in the paper he'd written, and he welcomed comments from other eye care professionals.

One of the possible reasons Robert put forth resulted from the fact that the average person blinks 20 thousand to 25 thousand times a day, and the rubbing of the contact lens might have some effect on the axial length of the eyeball. Perhaps the lens retarded the axial growth, which otherwise would have resulted in more myopia.

Another theory suggested the lenses were fitted flatter than the flattest reading obtained by the ophthalmometer which provided a slightly flatter front refracting surface. Or, perhaps the contact lens, being closer to the nodal point of the optical system of the eye, might result in less strain. In addition, glasses present spherical and other aberrations. The rigid contact lens might also cause a change, possibly chemical, to the pre-corneal film of the eye, or result in a different index of refraction or pH.

These suppositions and more were laid out in the article, which created a storm of interest, not just in the United States but around the globe. With 24 percent of the world's populace nearsighted, the idea that wearing hard lenses would stop its progression was phenomenal. Optometrists and ophthalmologists from all over responded to the possible 15 reasons that Robert put forward.

Robert's office mail tripled with letters from his peers who agreed or disagreed with his conclusions, as well as from patients who wanted more information. A large portion of the mail included comments from ophthalmologists and optometrists who were willing to agree with his conclusion but wanted to add their own theories as to which of Robert's reasons for the retardation of myopia might be the correct one.

Robert was amazed at the publicity he received as a result of the thesis. The National Eye Research Foundation sponsored a press conference to be held in New York City. All the major news magazines would be there.

Ruth's due date was fast approaching, but Robert thought he could make it to New York and back before she would go into labor. He wanted to be there for the birth but also wanted to talk about his theory. He was sure he could do both.

As he ran out the door to catch the train to the city, he told Ruth, "I'm going to New York so cross your legs. Don't have the baby without me!"

Robert gave the press conference. On the way back he was so eager to get home, he inadvertently missed a *Time* magazine photographer who was waiting at the station to get a photo. Robert had taken the freight elevator, a trick he knew well. This eye doctor, who'd just been interviewed by some of the world's greatest news magazines, had worked as a laborer on the railroad after high school, loading freight cars to build up his slender body.

The *Time* magazine article ran on November 15, 1957, explaining the theory about rigid contact lenses and its potential to retard the progression of myopia. A host of other articles followed, targeted to both eye care professionals and the general public. Since nearsightedness affects a large portion of the world's populace, the story went beyond the United States. One Associated Press story about Dr. Robert Morrison's myopia retardation via rigid lenses ran throughout the entire world. It made a major impression in Asia since myopia affects almost 60 percent of the Asian population.

Robert urged eye care professionals or scientists to perform controlled studies that could legitimize and validate the theory so that eye care professionals could have a solid basis for prescribing the rigid contact lens to children or teenagers. Two studies, one done at the College of Optometry at Indiana University and the other by an ophthalmologist in Bath, England, supported Robert's conclusion.

The theory was widely accepted but some practitioners strongly disagreed with it, as did a study done at the University of Singapore. Robert hoped that more extensive, federally funded studies would be done at more institutions in the United States. He wanted them to prove the theory in no uncertain terms, primarily to provide eye doctors with what Robert called the *moral right* to recommend rigid contact lenses for adolescents with myopia. After all, the lenses were more complex than simple eye glasses with a prescription for simple myopia, and were sometimes more costly. In addition, they required more daily care and attention than a pair of glasses.

Though Robert would continue to offer the rigid contact lens for patients who wanted it for vision and appearance, he wasn't comfortable recommending the use of the modality with the promise of retarding nearsightedness until it was supported by an official, properly controlled study.

Meanwhile, the waiting rooms of eye doctors all over the world became populated by children and their parents who didn't want to wait for absolute proof. If the children's prescriptions didn't change, not only would they maintain their vision at whatever point it had been when the rigid lens was prescribed, the children wouldn't have to continually buy stronger and stronger eyeglasses.

Parents and their offspring were seeking the rigid contact lens in an attempt to slow down the increasing nearsightedness. They believed in the theory, or at the very least, hoped the contact lens would improve vision without eyeglasses and might be of some benefit in limiting the myopia. As for the child or teenager, the fact that they didn't have to be *four eyes* was just an added benefit.

Whether or not Robert's theory was proven, it was a major impetus in the growth of rigid contact lens use. Later, the soft lens he helped develop would further the use of contact lenses, creating a booming industry that continues today.

# 4

## INVENTING AND DEVELOPING
## THE SOFT CONTACT LENS

P RAGUE, CZECHOSLOVAKIA'S CHARLES BRIDGE WAS AWASH
with the usual foot traffic on this early evening in 1961.
Prague workers were heading home or to their favorite pub to socialize over one of the city's famous Pilsner beers. Young couples
strolled hand-in-hand. European tourists walked slowly, stopping
periodically to admire the dramatic sculpted figures that lined both
sides along the bridge's full length.

Six centuries were captured on this bridge where the historic
statues carried a dark coating of soot from the city's coal furnaces.
The ash that settled into every fold of the ancient figures made
them seem all the more mysterious, especially at dusk when they
blended like ghosts into the night.

Normally, Robert Morrison would have admired the atmosphere and the panorama as the city lights blinked on. Tonight he
slowly walked toward his hotel, deep in thought, trying to fully
comprehend the amazing new ideas that were spinning around in
his head.

It just might work ... the material he'd just seen had staggering
potential.

He was returning from his first visit with Professor Otto Wichterle. The chemist had worked with Professor Lim here in Prague to create a new plastic gel. Robert recalled how he had heard about it through a telephone call from his good friend, Pierre Rocher, who headed the largest contact lens firm in France.

It had been early in the morning and Robert was busy with a patient at his office in New York when his receptionist told him he had a long distance call from Paris. Fortunately, one of his associates had been available to complete the patient's examination so Robert was able to speak to his friend.

"Pierre, this is a pleasant surprise."

"Bob, how are you? Are you working still on the improvements you wanted to make in the contact lenses?"

"You know me well!" he laughed. "Always."

"I was thinking that. And I said to myself that you should see a new plastic as soon as possible. It is hydrophilic."

Pierre pronounced the term in his soft French accent—"hide-droh-phileek"—but Robert immediately understood the point. A hydrophilic plastic was the opposite of the current hydrophobic plastic used in all rigid contact lenses. The *phobic* indicated the plastic would not adjust to an environment with water. A hydrophilic plastic liked water and would absorb some of it. It was an excellent choice for the liquid environment of the eye.

"Is your company working on this?" Robert asked. "They must be interested in the discovery."

Pierre's firm belonged to the largest optical company in France, and it had all the resources necessary to perform the research and development on the new plastic. What a coup it would be for anyone who was able to work on such an exciting development!

"We have discussed it, of course. Monsieur Grandperret and the others have no interest. However, chemists in Prague are working with it for many different things."

He paused briefly. "Bob, I know you are constantly looking

for better materials to make a contact lens. This is a fascinating material, one you should investigate. I will send you a copy of an article about it."

The article that Pierre had sent him had appeared in the prestigious journal *Lancet*. At first Robert was puzzled as to why Pierre had bothered to even send it to him. The article discussed an artificial mandible—a jawbone! What would that have to do with his interest in optics? Then he read the paper in detail and discovered that the artificial jawbone was made of an inert material that was compatible with human tissues. It was soft and could be sterilized.

That was exciting, of course. Even more important for optical purposes, the real magic was *clear*—quite literally. The material was crystal clear.

Robert read the article four times. He needed more information, and he was not one to sit and wait for what he wanted. Robert called the airline. Then he called Ruth and told her not to plan dinner. He'd just have enough time to throw some clothes in a bag.

By 8 p.m. that night, he was already on a flight from New York to Prague.


PROFESSOR OTTO WICHTERLE WORE A NEAT BUSINESS SUIT, WHICH surprised Robert, who was expecting a white lab coat. The professor was a thin man of medium height with a ruddy, uneven complexion. Robert's first impression was that the professor had a skin condition in the past which healed, but not well.

His warmth was genuine as he welcomed Robert with a firm handshake and, surprisingly, he welcomed him in English. At lunch in a small restaurant nearby, Robert was able to learn more personal details about the man himself, including the fact that he loved tennis, Robert's favorite sport.

Robert was impressed with the professor's grasp of chemistry and the power of the man's intelligence which extended to his command of languages. Besides Czech, the professor spoke German, Russian, and English. Not every language had been learned by choice. In 1939, Germany invaded Czechoslovakia. The professor's research had been interrupted when the Nazis closed the Czech universities during the war.

Czechoslovakia had later come under the sphere of Russian influence, but learning English was the professor's own idea. He had studied the language and used the radio he had at home to listen to the British Broadcasting Channel, the BBC, every night to perfect his ability to pronounce the language. Fortunately for Robert, the professor's diligence and aptitude for the English language made their working relationship and eventual friendship much easier.

By 1961 when Robert met Professor Wichterle, the Institute of Macromolecular Chemistry at the Czechoslovak Academy of Science was the professor's kingdom. It was clear that the other scientists and employees respected him and deferred to his decisions. Several years later, the professor was to lose his job as head of his own research institute when he participated in the Prague Spring uprising, a brief intellectual and artistic renaissance against hard-line Communist leaders that was put down and resulted in even greater Soviet influence.

That loss of his position due to politics, however, was still in his future. At this time when Robert first met him, Dr. Wichterle was mainly concerned with his newest invention and eager to share the possibilities with the optometrist from Pennsylvania in the United States.

Even though Professor Wichterle and his partner, Dr. Lim, were bright chemists, Robert soon discovered their knowledge of optics was limited. No wonder they had welcomed him so warmly.

The two scientists were more than happy to explain the new material to Robert and ask his advice on its potential in optometry. Professor Wichterle explained that the unique, new plastic was called hydroxyethylmethacrylate, or HEMA for short. The polymer was vastly different in substance from prior plastic materials. Its hydrophilic property, which had excited Robert when he learned of it, would enable the HEMA polymer to be used in ways that were not possible with current plastic technology. Professor Wichterle was already experimenting with the HEMA plastic for a host of different uses.

The question on Robert's mind was, "Could it be used in a contact lens?"

The professor answered unequivocally. "Yes, of course. It would be entirely possible to use it in a contact lens. In fact, I am already attempting to do so."

Professor Wichterle drove Robert to a small building where he was working to create the lenses. On the way, he explained that he had managed to make a spin cast machine that would take the liquified gel and form it into a curved contact lens. Although the professor's English was good, Robert was having difficulty understanding exactly what this machine he mentioned would do. No wonder! It turned out the equipment was made from an erector set like the one Robert had given his son, Jimmy, to play with over the holidays. The jury-rigged device sat on a hot plate, the coffee stains still visible on the outer edge. It was creative. It did the job. But, clearly, Professor Wichterle had improvised.

Robert studied the system that Professor Wichterle had set up in his laboratory. Despite any negative first impression, he realized that this device was no toy. It was a clever creation in which raw liquid HEMA polymer was introduced via a tube into a mold that was spinning. The mold was positioned on the hot plate. The heat was the catalyst that made the fluid solution turn into a gel.

The erector set—that was the term Robert applied to Professor Wichterle's unique creation—used a pulley-like system to spin the mold. Professor Wichterle had used a record player (he called it a gramophone player) to achieve the spinning phenomenon. It was clear to Robert that the professor was not only a genius but innovative.

As the liquid turned into a gel, the front side of the gelatinous material took the curvature of the mold; the back side became like a parabola. The technique worked centrifugally, like an electric mixer. The faster the mold would spin, the deeper the curve on the lens would become.

In creating a lens that would fit the eye and stay in place properly, it was necessary for the lens to slide minimally on the eye when blinking. That way, the lens would stay on the cornea, not slide off it.

To function properly, a contact lens must be fitted so that it will move slightly as the eye blinks. The cornea needs to receive some oxygen to avoid edema or swelling. The waste products are removed by the slight movement. The trick is to create the proper curvature so the lens moves just enough—but not so much that it slips around the eye excessively.

To find the correct curve of the lens, Professor Wichterle was using a hit-or-miss method. He would make a contact lens, have someone fit it onto the eye, and if it was too tight and did not move, he would make another lens and slow the spinning down. Using fewer revolutions per minute would create a flatter lens with less curvature. If the lens was too loose and therefore slipped downward when the eye blinked, it didn't stay on the cornea. In that case, Professor Wichterle would make another lens, but this time, he'd spin it faster to deepen the curve.

The system was primitive, but it worked for the time being—well enough, at least, for the professor to experiment with the technique using the new HEMA plastic gel.

More discomforting to Robert was the fact that the original lenses were kept in a glass vial, and the professor showed him how they could be removed with a glass cutter. Robert cringed at the thought that, however careful the person might be, tiny pieces of glass might adhere to the lens. He was sure that he could make the system more precise and efficient.

"Professor Wichterle, if this material could be cut with a lathe, you could make the contact lens spherical on both sides. It wouldn't be parabolic on one. It would be a better optical system."

"I think that is an interesting idea. I don't know that I can do that here, not so easily at least. And I do not know the optics like you do, Dr. Morrison. If I give you some of the HEMA polymer gel, perhaps you could try it."

Robert agreed immediately. He was getting a gift as good as any he'd ever received for a birthday. Professor Wichterle put some of the HEMA into a test tube, then broke the test tube to release the bar of gel. It was the size of a pen, and Robert guessed that he would be able to cut this amount into buttons that he could lathe into 10 to 15 lenses. He slid the small bar of gel into his briefcase, tucking it in a corner and protecting it with papers so it wouldn't slide around.

"I appreciate this, Professor. I will let you know how this works."

They shook hands on it.

Robert returned to his own lab in Harrisburg. So far, he had only made rigid contact lenses. With this new HEMA polymer material, he could make softer contact lenses that would permit longer wear. They would be more comfortable as well as more convenient.

His contact lens laboratory in Harrisburg was already set up and included all the equipment necessary to create rigid contact lenses. Robert simply adapted it and began to experiment with the new HEMA polymer.

Ironically, as he was working on the project, he received a letter from Dr. William Policoff, an optometrist in Wilkes Barre, Pennsylvania. In part, the letter stated, "This material will make a fine diaphragm for women to use as a contraceptive device but will never make a contact lens."

Over the next several months, Robert tried various techniques and methods for preparing the HEMA gel and creating a contact lens that would be of the right size and shape. He discovered that the hardened gel could be cut easily with diamond tools. The only trouble was he couldn't polish the resulting contact lens, and therefore he wasn't able to remove the lathe marks. The usual polishes used for rigid contact lenses were two chemicals that were mixed with water, tin oxide and zinc oxide, but the water-based polish made the lenses gummy so he couldn't use them to polish out the lathe marks.

He began cutting the contact lenses more carefully and avoided polishing them. Done this way, the lathe marks were so fine that they would not cause any problems for the wearer's cornea. At that point he began fitting the soft lenses on volunteers' eyes in Harrisburg.

One day, while he was lecturing to a group of optometrists and ophthalmologists in Philadelphia, Robert mentioned the problem of polishing the lathe marks away. Even though his technique resulted in such fine lines that they caused no problem, it was a detail that he still wanted to perfect.

A hand shot up from one corner of the room. "Dr. Morrison, why don't you polish the lens with oil instead of water-based polishing material?"

Robert filed the idea away in his mind. It made perfect sense. When he returned to the lab, he bought simple vegetable oil from the local supermarket and tried it. The oil worked perfectly, erasing the lathe marks. He tried 3-IN-ONE oil as well, which also worked. The lenses came out smooth and clear.

To this day, many soft contact lens labs still lathe the lenses. With improvements, the newer lathes cut so finely that polishing is either eliminated or done more quickly and easily.

Rᴏʙᴇʀᴛ ᴊᴏᴜʀɴᴇʏᴇᴅ ᴛᴏ Pʀᴀɢᴜᴇ ᴏꜰᴛᴇɴ, ᴅɪsᴄᴜssɪɴɢ ʜɪs ᴘʀᴏɢʀᴇss with Professor Wichterle. One day at lunch, the two men sat in a small restaurant made cozy against the dreary winter day by heavy velvet drapes.

Robert was impressed by Professor Wichterle's intelligence, but the professor knew little about optics.

"I am a chemist," he'd say. "But I want to learn."

Robert took another spoonful of the chicken soup. It was rich and flavorful. He was enjoying the lunch as much as the discussion.

Well, perhaps not as much. He enjoyed discussing optics with the professor because the man's quick mind absorbed the information and was able to offer other perspectives. During their discussions, Robert often struggled learning some of the chemistry Professor Wichterle talked about. He wished he'd paid more attention during his chemistry classes in school.

Robert happened to mention to the professor that he and his staff in Harrisburg were storing the lenses in water. The professor mulled this over and looked at his own soup for a moment. Salty soup, Robert realized later, but whether that had anything to do with the professor's thought process, he'd never know.

"Perhaps normal saline would be better. It is more close to tears, with salt."

"You're right. I should have thought of that."

When he returned home, Robert immediately visited the Polyclinic Hospital in Harrisburg and requested a jug of normal saline, the type used for injections.

He soaked the lens he'd made in the saline and called one of his patients who had often tried out new lenses for him. It would be the first experiment with the new technique. Robert made sure that his test subject, a man named Jerry, was at ease with trying the new lens, though he didn't expect any problems.

They inserted the lens that had been soaked in saline.

"How's it feel?"

"It's OK. Doesn't seem to be moving, though."

Robert had taught Jerry how easily the contact could be removed by merely sliding it to one side and lightly pinching it.

"Maybe it needs a flatter curve. Take it out. I'll take a look at it."

Jerry tried to pop out the lens. "I can't seem to get it out."

"Let me see." Robert moved closer and examined the lens. He didn't know why Jerry was having a problem, but he expected to remove the lens easily.

It didn't budge. Robert tried everything, but the lens adhered tightly.

He was trying to think of what he could do when his secretary called to him. "Dr. Morrison, you have a phone call from Mexico."

"I can't take it now, Colleen. Tell whoever it is that I'll call back." Robert turned back to the problem with the contact lens. This was serious. Robert didn't often panic, but his stomach lurched at the thought of a lens stuck on his cornea.

Thirty seconds later Colleen was back. "Dr. Morrison, it's Dr. Korder in Mexico City. He's got a problem and needs to talk to you right away."

Robert felt like muttering, *I've got my own problem*, but he was trying to remain calm for Jerry's sake. No use in panicking his patient, who, in any case, was already aware of the problem.

"Dr. Korder insists, Doctor. He's practically screaming."

"What's he saying?"

"I don't know. He's yelling in Spanish."

Robert sighed. Korder was the manager of the Morrison Laboratories in Mexico. The man knew English but became emotional in Spanish. What the hell could the problem be?

"Let me have the phone. Jerry, just sit here and relax. I'll be right back."

Robert took the call. He did his best to hurry but it took fifteen minutes.

He returned to the lab, his mind reeling with ways to deal with the recalcitrant contact lens. He tried to push the thought from his brain that he would surely denude Jerry's corneal epithelium. His brow grew damp at the thought.

He tried another time to remove the lens. It was loose. One more try and it popped out. Jerry gave the doctor a relieved look and another look that Robert assumed meant, "That's the last time I'm going to be your guinea pig."

Jerry looked as though he was ready to bolt. Robert thought for a moment, then he said, "Just stay here, Jerry. I'll be right back."

He left Jerry sitting in the chair and rushed to the nearest pool supply store where he bought a pH meter. He tested the saline he'd gotten in the hospital. It had a pH of 5.5. He reviewed the salinity of tears. Normally, they would have a pH of 7.4.

He had been adding N-vinyl pyrrolidone to make the water content higher in the lens (55% compared to the Czech 38%). The increased water content would make the lens slightly stiffer, giving better optical quality so the patient would hopefully see better. However, the HEMA gel had then become pH sensitive. He now knew he had to increase the alkalinity in the contact lens solution.

This was the birth of an enormous business. Eventually, contact lens solutions were all buffered to provide a pH of over seven, usually 7.4. A simple solution of water, salt, and a buffer compound cost just pennies, but the contact lens solutions were selling for several dollars.

Robert wasn't concerned with that at the moment. He was too excited with what he'd accomplished in adapting the HEMA gel with water and managing to lathe and polish it. The soft contact lens was now a viable product for millions of people. The potential profit was beyond Robert's wildest dreams, but he wasn't a greedy man.

Perhaps that was why he underestimated the potential for greed in others.

# 5

## RECEIVING THE PATENT RIGHTS
## FOR THE HEMA GEL

T HE PHONE RANG IN THE HARRISBURG HOME THAT ROBERT and Ruth had built on the property he'd shown her when they first met. The *bachelor pad* was now designed for their young family. When Robert picked up the receiver, he expected his sister or one of his employees to be on the other line. Instead, the unfamiliar caller introduced himself as Martin Pollock.

"I'm a patent attorney with the National Patent Development Company. I met Dr. Wichterle in Prague."

Martin Pollock went on to explain he'd been in Russia in order to get the license for a new machine that made pleasant sounds designed to put insomniacs to sleep. On the way back to New York, he had stopped in Prague.

"The doctor and his compatriots think very highly of you, Dr. Morrison."

"I'm glad to hear that."

"I took the liberty of also phoning Phil Salvatore. He owns the contact lens lab, Obrig Laboratories. Mr. Salvatore also spoke well of you. You have an excellent reputation."

"I hope so. I've worked hard to be very good at what I do."

"Obviously, Doctor, you have accomplished it. And now I understand Dr. Wichterle is going to assign the patents for his HEMA plastic to you."

"That's my understanding, yes."

"Our company, National Patent Development, represents major names in business—Westinghouse, GE—and we are experts on Eastern European patent rights. I'd like to discuss how we might work with you."

"What did you have in mind, Mr. Pollock?"

"I'd very much like to meet with you to discuss how National Patent Development might help you."

Robert knew his strength was in optics and creativity. The business details of bringing what he saw as a major advance in lens technology to the marketplace were foreign to him. He could use help in making the most of the products he could develop.

"I'm always willing to listen. I'll be in New York in a few days. Can we meet then?"


MARTIN POLLOCK'S OFFICE WAS SMALL BUT IMPRESSIVE WITH WOOD finished furnishings and the obvious air of a New York designer's touch. The man himself was similar to Robert's 5' 9" height, though he was a bit heavier than Robert. He often smoked a pipe.

Pollock made the usual greetings and led the way to a conference room. He pulled a large bundle of letters from his briefcase and spread them out on the long mahogany table in front of Robert. The letterheads were from large companies.

"Dr. Morrison, these letters are from major clients. We're happy to say that we have several." He gave a nervous laugh that seemed out of place. Robert noticed it, but he had met people who were uncomfortable when they first met someone. He suspected Pollock wasn't at ease.

"Large as many of these companies are, they cannot do business in the Eastern Bloc without expert help. They do things differently there than in the United States or even Western Europe."

"I imagine so," Robert affirmed.

Even though Dr. Wichterle and some of his companions spoke English, the communist system was vastly different from what Robert was familiar with in the United States—and he wasn't that familiar with the U.S. legal and marketing systems, either. He was an optometrist, not a patent attorney.

"That's where I come in. I'd like to help you in your dealings in Eastern Europe, and I have a proposal."

Pollock proceeded to explain what his company had in mind. He wanted to structure a patent agreement in which Robert would pay the Czech government one dollar for the patent rights for each lens sold. The Czechs, in turn, would pay National Patent Development Company five cents for each lens. Pollock explained that the deal was far from being done, but he wanted very much to work with Robert on the project.

Despite the occasional high-pitched laugh that Robert attributed to nerves or just an odd habit, Pollock seemed professional. Though he didn't actually read the reference letters, the corporate letterheads were impressive, as was the well located Park Avenue office that was small but plush. The opportunity to have professional help in bringing the new products made from the HEMA gel to market convinced Robert to hire the firm as his patent development attorneys. He was later to call himself incredibly naive.

A FEW MONTHS LATER, ROBERT WAS ENJOYING DINNER AT PROFESSOR Wichterle's home in Prague. In working together to develop the HEMA gel and discussing optics, the two men had become friendly, and they respected each other's talents. Robert was enjoying the meal of sausage and sauerkraut when Otto spoke.

"Robert, I have decided that I must give the patent rights to the gel to someone who can use them in the Western Hemisphere. Perhaps some other areas as well."

Robert put down his fork and looked across the table at the professor. If Professor Wichterle gave the patent rights to anyone but Robert, it would affect Robert's experiments tremendously. He could lose all control of the HEMA or else the cost of licensing it would be prohibitive to his developing a soft contact lens from the material.

"Otto, I want to be able to continue experimenting with the gel. I've made quite a bit of progress so far."

"Of course, Robert. That is why you are one of my top choices."

Robert was pleased to know that he was one of the choices, but that also meant there were several other contenders.

"I know you must give this careful thought, Otto. May I ask, who else are you considering?"

"The company Bausch & Lomb seemed interested. But, of course, your agent, Dr. Allen Isen, was here and we discussed how he could work on the project as well. I did as you requested and showed him in detail how to make the hydrophilic gel."

"*My agent?*"

Robert was puzzled. He had met Allen Isen in business dealings because Isen owned the Frontier Contact Lens Company in Buffalo, but he didn't know how Isen had even known about the gel in order to contact Wichterle.

"Otto, this is out of left field. Allen Isen is not my agent."

"But, Robert, he said that you sent him here. Also, that he knew you were being represented by Mr. Pollock and Mr. Feldman." The professor didn't blink. It seemed normal to him. Those capitalistic Americans were always working on one project or another, always bringing in other partners.

Robert sensed a ball of yarn was unraveling before his eyes. Pollock and Feldman had not mentioned that Allen Isen would be involved. They hadn't bothered to tell him that they were sending anyone to Prague. Worse, the casual way that Professor Wichterle had mentioned he'd shown and explained everything about the new gel to this relative stranger, Allen Isen, told Robert that something was wrong.

Suddenly he wondered if all his work was in danger,

He repeated once more that Allen Isen was not his representative and then his concerns boiled over and he said pointblank, "It's very important to me that I have the patent rights to the HEMA gel, Otto."

"I know, my friend. I think I would like you to have them, but I must consider the best person to make use of the material and to market it."

"I understand completely."

The concern in Robert's voice contradicted his words. Professor Wichterle tried to ease his mind.

"Don't worry, Robert. I will make the decision carefully, but I must meet with this Allen Isen and some others. I will go to the United States soon in order to do so, and then I will decide."

Apparently the strain showed on Robert's face. If he didn't get the patent rights, then his chances of working with the new plastic were close to nil. He had already invested so much time in the project, but even more important was the emotional involvement. He'd thought of the soft lens development as his special baby, and he wanted to bring it to the world.

"Robert, you must understand that this is just a necessity, something I must do in order to explore the options and make a proper decision. In fact, I will tell you a little secret. You are my first choice."

Professor Wichterle smiled.


A MONTH LATER, PROFESSOR WICHTERLE VISITED ROBERT IN HARrisburg on a trip to the United States that included his visit to see Allen Isen. By this point Martin Pollock had explained that he'd sent Isen to Prague in order to gather more information for the patent investigation and marketing.

He explained to Robert, "I didn't think you'd mind, since we're all working together and Isen is one of our experts on the Eastern Bloc." He did apologize for not telling Robert what he'd planned. He was so apologetic that Robert calmed down and ignored a nagging sense of uneasiness.

To Robert's great relief and joy, Professor Wichterle eventually decided Robert would be the recipient of the patent rights for the HEMA gel. It was a wonderful opportunity, and Robert was extremely relieved that his concern had been unfounded. He'd earned the patent rights.

Unfortunately, Professor Wichterle's intelligence did not extend to an understanding of the American capacity for legal chicanery ... neither did Robert's.

# 6

## WORLD HEALTH ORGANIZATION TOUR

O VER THE 15 YEARS ROBERT HAD BEEN WORKING TO IMPROVE eye sight, he'd received countless letters from around the world—letters sent from individual physicians, hospitals, clinics, and charities—each of them asking the famous eye doctor to speak at a meeting or conference. Robert always preached to his students that every letter deserves an answer. He replied to each invitation to speak, even if it just included a thank-you and a brief message that perhaps he'd be able to visit their country someday. Then he relegated them to a file drawer in his office. But never the circular file.

Though his practice kept him occupied in Harrisburg and New York, he was too polite to simply throw away what to the writer was an important invitation. The host of invitations and the idea of visiting some of the locations percolated in the back of his mind, but he was simply too busy to seriously consider taking on every speaking engagement requested.

He was also still dealing with some serious issues in arranging his recent gain of patent rights for the new HEMA gel—an ongoing legal hassle that was essential, but took more time than he wanted. Though Robert was a trusting man, he was still uneasy about problems in owning the patent rights.

Meanwhile, Robert continued the activities involved in his regular eye care practice. His reputation as an expert had grown, and the office was extremely busy. He was doing better financially than he'd ever dreamed possible. The Morrison practice now included five optometrists and two ophthalmologists on the staff. The growth had been phenomenal, and the practice was well on its way to what would eventually make it the largest ethical eye care practice in the United States.

Robert had a tendency to ignore the financial success he had achieved. He left all the details of running the office to Peggy, who was thrilled at the success of the practice and never failed to make comparisons and comments.

"Did you know we had a great month, nearly double last year?"

Robert realized this was exciting to her, but he had to make an effort to listen and make an appropriate comment. He was really not interested. He'd rather work with the patients and continue learning and developing new techniques. The financial gains were Peggy's business and merely a side result of his simply doing the job he loved the best way possible.

In addition, he was intent on giving back. One evening, he took the folder of invitations to speak out of the file drawer, sat down, and started to read each one. The locations read like an atlas of the world, and many of them sounded like exotic destinations to a man born and raised in Pennsylvania. The letters came from Asia, Africa, Eastern and Western Europe, from countries including Russia, Hong Kong, and India.

Something about a letter from the Gandhi Eye Hospital in India caught his attention. Serious eye problems were especially common in India, and Robert knew he could make a major difference there. He'd always had the desire to see that the less fortunate people of the world could have their vision corrected.

He was convinced that better vision was the secret to changing many people's lives. Children could see a chalkboard to learn. A husband and father could improve his vision enough to drive, earn a living, and have some self-respect. A mother could sew for her children or to earn extra income.

Robert cleared his desk and laid the letters out, sorting them by location, playing mind games. If he went to each place he'd been invited to, Robert would be speaking and teaching his way around the world.

AT THE TIME, ROBERT WAS GIVING A COURSE IN FITTING CONTACT lenses. It covered everything from beginning eye care and exam techniques to correcting astigmatism and presbyopia. The course discussed leaving lenses on the eye for weeks and months and the need to maintain corneal integrity. He'd taught hundreds of optometrists and ophthalmologists in these courses, which had been approved by the government. Consequently, many of the attendees at the week-long course were Army and Navy doctors. The courses were conducted at his offices in Harrisburg, and it seemed they were becoming increasingly popular.

Robert wanted to ensure that the doctors would know a good contact lens from a poor one, and they could study any effect, adverse or not, that a contact lens might have on the eye or eyelids. They were taught how to consider each and every factor that affected the quality and the functionality of a contact lens, including internal stress, warpage, proper thickness for the power of the lens, and edge contour. He wanted to be helpful, and at the same time, he wanted the others to take pride in their work.

Always the genial host, Robert would end the course on Friday evenings with a dinner for the attendees in his home, which included thick, juicy steaks and good wine. Ruthie, sometimes with Patty's help, did most of the work putting the wonderful dinner together. Years later, Robert would still run into some of the people who had enjoyed those dinners, and he insisted many of them remembered Ruthie's delicious dinners more than anything they'd learned during the courses he'd taught.

One of the students in the current course was Dr. Seymour Sweet, an outgoing fellow from Tulsa, Oklahoma. He came up to Robert after one class during which Robert had mentioned that the courses would be suspended for a few months since he would be traveling. Robert told them about his plan to work his way around the world, lecturing and providing free consultations and contact lenses to the indigent.

"Dr. Morrison, I'd like to accompany you on the trip."

"It's a lecture circuit, really. I don't have the option of taking anyone with me."

"I'd pay my own way, of course. But the experience would be amazing. I'd really like to join you. I can help you in some of the free consultations."

Robert didn't want to insult the man, but certain groups had invited *him*, and he wasn't sure if they'd take another doctor. "Sy, I really don't need an assistant."

"Please think about it. This would be an incredible experience. I'll do whatever it takes to join you. I'll carry your bags." He grinned.

Robert had always called himself a complete and utter pushover for anyone who asked any favor of him. He almost always gave in. This request was no exception. He really didn't need another doctor for the work, but he rationalized that Seymour was an entertaining fellow, and on the long journey it would be good to have the companionship.

"I'll do the lectures, but you can help with the charity fittings."

"It's a deal." They shook on it.

———

Robert arranged a meeting with representatives of the World Health Organization to discuss plans for the trip. The schedule was organized as best it could be by arranging locations and suggested dates so the trip could take place in a logical sequence. The U.S. Information Agency would notify each country of his date of arrival. The World Health Organization decided to kick off the tour with a reception provided by UNICEF (The United Nations Children's Fund). That was the start of the tour that would eventually take Sy and Robert across the globe in three months.

They began traveling west in the United States, stopping along the way at the University of Michigan, heading from there to the University of California at Berkeley, then on to Hawaii, Hong Kong, and Japan.

In Hong Kong, Robert met Dr. Rita Ng and her husband who were then planning to move to Toronto, Canada. They explained to Robert that they loved the free enterprise system of Hong Kong and wanted to live in a democratic country. The idea of Chinese mainlanders ruling them was not one they could adapt to.

The couple was looking forward to an interesting discussion with the American doctor. They invited Robert to have a special dinner at their apartment, which turned out to be beautifully furnished and it sat high on a hill overlooking the city. The meal included a delicacy which the couple passed to their guest with great pride—1,000-year-old eggs. The name made Robert think the worst.

Dr. Ng bent toward Robert and whispered, "They're not *really* 1,000 years old, only perhaps a month or two."

Robert tried not to gag. Dr. Ng soon explained that the eggs were raw duck eggs that had been buried in the ground. They were coated with clay and other materials which would supposedly preserve them, something Robert didn't particularly want to think about. Then the eggs were dug up and carved into neat slices as a special dish for guests.

Robert nibbled a piece of one. The flavor was pungent, almost cheese-like, but he had trouble getting over the name itself, and the eggs didn't appeal to him. His mind wandered to thoughts of bacteria and fungus, though he politely pretended he enjoyed the dish.

The next day Robert visited the Kwong Wah Hospital in Hong Kong where he lectured, and afterwards, fitted a hundred Chinese children with contact lenses. The children all had congenital cataracts. Robert explained to Sy that the children had had cataract surgery, but they still needed very thick glasses. They had light perception but no real useable vision.

What bothered Robert most was the fact that not even one of the children had glasses, much less glasses that would be able to improve their vision to an acceptable level. Apparently money was the problem. Regular glasses were too costly for these people, and the thick cataract glasses these children needed were even more expensive.

Robert was sure that contact lenses would work far better for the children's problem. Of course, finding the money to provide the lenses was still an issue.

Robert and Sy decided to provide the fittings for the lenses, then donated the aphakic contact lenses to the children by mailing them at no charge from the Morrison Lab in Harrisburg to Hong Kong. When asked who had provided this largesse, Robert simply said that the CITE Foundation (Conservation and Improvement of the Eye Foundation) was paying for the lenses, and the hospital should thank *them*, not him.

The front page of the major newspaper, the *Hong Kong Standard*, wrote an article about the program. Meanwhile, the head of Kwong Wah Hospital wrote a special thank-you letter to the CITE Foundation, expounding on the hospital's gratitude to the organization. What they didn't know was—Robert *was* the CITE

Foundation.

THE CITE FOUNDATION DIRECTORS WERE REVEREND SHERIDAN Watson Bell, a prominent protestant clergyman at Grace Methodist Church in Harrisburg, and Dr. Thomas Burns, a local obstetrician. They were unpaid advisors, but having them allowed Robert to have a state-recognized foundation. Of course, the organization was a front for Robert's charity so it seldom had any money in the bank.

However, one time Bill Cosby visited Harrisburg to see Robert, and he brought his five children along. During his visit, Cosby insisted on making a donation to a cause that Robert supported. Robert suggested a donation to the CITE Foundation to which Cosby generously contributed.

Robert and Cosby's mutual love was tennis, and they set up a doubles match with Robert's brother Vic and Dr. Minster Kunkle, general surgeon and then president of Harrisburg Hospital. After the match, the four were showering and Bill Cosby described how he managed to create his serve, which Robert had admired. Cosby used athletic gestures to explain how he threw the ball forward and brought his shoulder through. Afterwards, Cosby lunched at Robert's home.

The next day, Robert's son, Jim, was allowed to drive Bill Cosby to Bethlehem, Pennsylvania, in Queen Juliana's Rolls-Royce. Cosby had been invited there to address the students at Lehigh University.

WHEN THEY GOT TO TOKYO, ROBERT VISITED THE TOKYO CONTACT Lens Company. The offices were lavish, and as Robert admired them, he got a huge surprise. In the lobby, he was greeted by— himself! A picture of Dr. Robert Morrison had been hung on the wall of the reception room. Later, the manager told Robert that he was considered the patron saint of contact lenses.

Robert was scheduled to lecture at three places in India—Calcutta, Bombay, and a small town near New Delhi called Aligarh. In October of 1963, Robert and Sy arrived in New Delhi. A doctor from the Gandhi Eye Hospital picked them up at the airport and drove them to their hotel.

The hotel was elegantly furnished. Robert and Sy checked into their rooms, and a uniformed bellman showed Robert to his room with the usual pomp and circumstance of a first class hotel. No sooner had the door closed behind him, when a mouse scurried across the floor.

Robert phoned the front desk and told them he had an uninvited roommate.

"What do you expect us to do?" came the answer.

"I'd like you to remove the mouse at once."

A uniformed employee came to the room and asked where the creature was.

"Apparently under the bed."

The employee shook the bedspread and the frightened critter ran across the room. Nonchalantly, the man took a handkerchief from his pants pocket, dropped it over the running mouse, scooped up the handkerchief with the mouse in it, and carried the tidy package out of the room.


In India, Robert's lectures dealt with the eye condition called keratoconus, in which the clear cornea becomes thin and protrudes. The condition causes serious distortion of visual images, greatly impeding vision. Medicines can't help, but most cases can be treated with specially designed contact lenses. If a case is particularly bad, the patient might require a corneal transplant.

Robert was always fascinated with keratoconus, and he challenged himself to find a better way to help those with the disease.

Once someone asked him if he'd ever retire, and he replied, "I don't think so, but if I did, I would continue in practice but limit it to keratoconus patients."

While teaching ophthalmology at the Penn State University College of Medicine, Robert concluded that the excellent rigid lenses that had changed the life of many keratoconus patients, giving them useable, often excellent vision—might actually be exacerbating the formation of scar tissue on the cornea. He'd noted some scar tissue on many who'd never worn contact lenses, and he felt that the problem was worsened when individuals wore a rigid, constantly rubbing, contact lens.

Robert wrote a paper on the topic, which was published in the prestigious journal *Contemporary Ophthalmology*. In the paper, he presented his theory and suggested a solution to the problem which involved combining a soft lens to be worn on the cornea, in tandem with a rigid lens to decrease the rubbing effect. The soft lens could not be spherical, but instead, needed to be cylindrical (toric) curvature. The use of a soft spherical lens, often called a piggy back arrangement, had generally failed in the past, and Robert believed it was due to the fact that the lens was spherical.

After the paper was published, it received a great deal of attention. Robert hoped that it would result in keratoconic patients avoiding or delaying corneal transplantation.


ROBERT HAD BEEN INVITED TO SPEAK AT THE CONTACT LENS CENTRE at the Gandhi Eye Hospital in Aligarh, India. It had been established in 1957 to provide contact lenses to visually handicapped persons who could not benefit from any medical or surgical treatment.

The hospital itself had been founded in 1928 as a charitable institution by Dr. Mohanlal, an ophthalmologist of international repute. It contained 450 beds, with an eye bank, a school of optometry, a school of orthoptics, a contact lens department, X ray department, and other specialized clinics.

Unfortunately, someone had passed on the news that the famous American eye doctor was going to be at the Gandhi Eye Hospital and contact lenses would be provided at no charge. The article appeared in the newspapers, but in the confusion, the writer forgot to mention that the program was specifically designed to help patients who had keratoconus.

By the time Robert arrived, the line—which everyone was calling a *queue*, from the British term used in India—seemed to stretch from the front door of the hospital to the horizon.

The chief of ophthalmology appeared at the door with a sling on his arm, which he'd broken just that morning. This, Robert was to find out later, was the result of the chief's losing a game of *chicken* that day. It was part of Robert's cultural education to discover that many roads in India were just one lane. That fact did nothing to diminish the speed at which most Indians drove. When two cars going in the opposite direction would meet head-on, one would swerve off the road and the other would keep on going. Leaving the road was chicken, but it at least had the benefit of saving someone's life.

At the moment, though, the chief of ophthalmology was more concerned about the lines snaking down the street outside the hospital. The crowd of people seeking eye care was far larger than anyone had anticipated. He asked Robert for a suggestion.

"How many slit lamps do you have?" Robert asked. A slit lamp is a biomicroscope that turns sideways with a powerful beam of light that is narrowed to a mere slit. The instrument is most important in examining the eye and commonly found in every ophthalmologist and optometrist's office.

"Three," the chief told Robert.

"I'll speak for about an hour or so on how to diagnose the disease. Then we'll enlist more ophthalmologists to help us spend the morning screening and looking for those who have keratoconus."

Robert and Sy performed the eye screenings. When they broke for lunch, they met an American visitor, not a physician but a consultant, who was working at the hospital temporarily. As they were walking down the hall, he whispered to Robert a word of warning.

"Yes, this is a hospital, but whatever you do, do not eat a thing. Ask for a Coca Cola, and be sure to wipe the mouth of the bottle with your shirt tail. Do not use a glass, and above all, do not use the ice!"

Out of all the patients they saw that day, Robert and the group of eye professionals assisting him discovered 23 cases of keratoconus. They fitted each of the patients with special contact lenses Robert ordered from his home laboratory. The lenses were then sent to the hospital in India, where they were donated to the children.

While Robert was busy examining patients and coping with unfamiliar surroundings in India, he had no idea that events at home had taken a serious turn.

# 7

# A NIGHT IN
# A RUSSIAN JAIL

E ARLY THE NEXT MORNING, THE AMERICAN EMBASSY telephoned Robert in Aligarh, India, with the news that his father had died. It devastated him. He'd loved and admired the man, and here he was, thousands of miles and several plane connections away from home and family.

While he was still trying to deal with this shock, Robert received an invitation from a wealthy man who was known for his beautiful home not far from the hospital. The man had prepared a party featuring Indian curry dishes which he wished to share with the American doctor. Robert told him he was sorry, but he couldn't go to the party due to the terrible news about his father. Attending a party was the last thing on his mind.

The hospital representatives told Robert that the man was very important to their fundraising efforts and had donated great sums of money to help their patients. They urged Robert to attend the event and avoid disappointing their benefactor, suggesting it might even be a distraction from his grief.

After some coaxing, Robert agreed to go, but his heart wasn't in it. He barely tasted anything, and though he tried to socialize as best he could, he was merely going through the motions. His mind was in a fog.

Robert returned by automobile to New Delhi that evening with the small group from the hospital on the one-lane, paved road, constantly looking for objects in the way, namely cows. The huge beasts would wander onto the roads and were a danger to themselves and to the traffic. The cows in India were considered holy, never to be eaten, and in most cases, they were permitted to roam freely. Hitting one with a vehicle was not only bad form due to the damage to a sacred cow, but it could cause considerable damage to a vehicle and its passengers.

In New Delhi, Robert telephoned his parents' home and spoke to a friend who assured him that the funeral would go on, and his flying home would be fruitless. It would take a day or two for him to get there, and by then the service would be over.

Robert also received a telegram from his older brother, Alan, in which he advised Robert to avoid feeling badly about whatever decision he made, whether to fly home immediately or to stay and complete his speaking tour.

"If you want to give up the trip and your work and come home, that is the right thing to do. If you want to continue your work, then that is the right thing to do. Whatever you decide is the right thing to do."

Robert wondered if he would ever have the wisdom to send such a message. As Robert mulled it over, Sy Sweet sat nearby and asked, "Do you feel like crying?"

"Yes," Robert admitted.

"Then just let go."

He did.

The next morning, Dr. Vered, who did a lot of work with contact lenses in the area, came by the hotel to pick up Robert for the drive to the Gandhi Eye Hospital in Aligarh, about an hour's drive from New Delhi. They chatted at the hotel first, and Robert learned that the doctor's family had a hospital which was staffed only by family, and it did exclusively eye work and obstetrics. All the men were either ophthalmologists or optometrists, and all the women were obstetricians. One of the men was about to marry a girl who was not an obstetrician. Therefore, she was to go straight to medical school—at once—rather than break the family tradition.

Robert mentioned that he wanted to shop a bit that day to find some gifts for his wife, kids, and his mother. Dr. Vered pulled out his wallet and took out a big wad of Indian paper money, shoving the handful of rupees into Robert's hand.

"I would like you to use this to purchase some gifts for your family."

"No, I wouldn't think of it."

"I insist. It would be an honor for me to have you shop for your family."

"I appreciate that and thank you, but I can't accept this kindness."


ROBERT'S ACTIVITIES AND HIS DEDICATION DIDN'T GO UNNOTICED AT the Gandhi Eye Hospital. M.K. Gupta, chief medical officer of the hospital, drafted a letter which he sent to President John F. Kennedy praising Dr. Morrison and Dr. Sweet as examples of "what a doctor, sincere in his purpose, firm in determination, and zealous for selfless service, could achieve."

Several years later, a curator in Washington, D.C., telephoned Robert to inform him that a group was collecting mail and other memorabilia from the last 100 days of the Kennedy presidency in order to create a historical collection, and the letter to President Kennedy would be part of it.


AFTER INDIA, ROBERT AND SY WENT ON TO SOUTH AFRICA FOR MORE lectures. Finally, they landed in Russia. That year, 1963, was a time of distrust and friction between the United States and the USSR.

In preparation for the lecture tour, Robert had studied Russian by hiring a Russian Orthodox priest who visited his office in Harrisburg each morning before the business day began. Robert had also purchased tapes and a pillow speaker that would allow him to listen to the language tapes while sleeping. He'd once read that subliminal learning was the best, so he decided to test that claim. He tucked the speaker under his pillow and listened to a tape as he slept.

Once the pillow speaker fell out from under Robert's pillow and ended up under Ruthie's pillow. The next morning Ruthie awakened and said, "Dobre utro," which means *good morning* in Russian.

Apparently, some of it sunk in for Robert, too, because the Russian Orthodox priest who was acting as Robert's tutor finally asked him during one lesson, "Are you sure you have not been to Russia?"

Robert assured him he had not set foot in the country, but he was preparing for a trip with some language tapes. Then he asked why the priest was so sure he'd been in Russia.

"Because I am from Kiev and am trying to teach you as I speak, but you keep saying things with a Moscow accent!"

Robert explained that the language tapes he'd been using had been recorded by a Moscow teacher.

At any rate, Robert was eager to practice his Moscow-accented language skills. His efforts led to a frightening experience that could have kept Sy and him in a Russian prison for more years than they wanted to count.

As Robert and Sy were settling down at a dinner table in the Hotel Metropole's restaurant in Moscow, Robert noticed an opportunity to practice his Russian language skills. Two men were dining at the adjacent table. One of them was wearing an incredible Russian fur hat, much like the Persian lamb hats the women were wearing in the United States at the time.

Robert politely complimented the man's hat, telling him that it was a "pretty hat" in Russian. The man understood the stilted language that Robert spoke and politely thanked him.

Robert didn't want the opportunity to practice Russian to pass, so he extended the innocent conversation by asking what was good to eat at the restaurant. The man replied that he enjoyed the caviar and borsht, the dark red cabbage soup.

That was as far as the conversation got. Two policemen grabbed Robert, one by each arm, and pulled him out the door, his feet barely touching the ground, into a waiting car. Two other policemen were doing the same with Sy. The last two policeman took the Russian man Robert had been talking to.

The two eye doctors were taken to a police station where a jail cell was waiting for them. Five interrogators, in teams of two and three, asked questions of both men throughout the night. The police separated Robert and Sy and questioned each of them individually. As they were leading Sy away from him, Robert shouted out, "Only tell the truth and we will be saying the same thing!"

Later, Sy told Robert that he was relieved he'd yelled that instruction since he'd been thinking about making up a great story about how the two of them loved communism. He was prepared to say anything that occurred to him if he felt it might help them get released.

The two men had difficulty at first comprehending why they had been arrested. The policemen merely told them that they had spoken to the stranger at the restaurant. Obviously, to the policemen at least, that somehow meant they were planning some activity against the USSR.

When they'd first arrived at the police station, the officers had taken Robert's Minox camera, a camera so small, Robert was concerned they'd think it was a spy device. They also confiscated his cash which amounted to $974.

Robert felt the money belt on his trousers, with the secret, zipped compartment on the inside. It held three, one hundred dollar bills. Robert didn't mention the money belt, planning to say he'd forgotten about it if the police happened to find it. He hoped they wouldn't, because it had already occurred to him the money might be used as a bribe since the Russians loved U.S. dollars.

Robert understood the Russian language, but he wasn't skilled enough to debate with the Russian policemen. Between halting English and his Russian, though, he managed to converse. The interrogators asked Robert to sign a confession that he and Sy were plotting something against the Russian government with the man who'd been at the next table in the restaurant.

"Honest to God, we had no such plans. We just wanted to be friendly to the man."

That man had also been arrested, though Robert hadn't a clue what had become of him. He never saw him at the police station. Robert repeated his story to the interrogators—that he'd simply commented on the hat to the Russian and asked him about the food.

One interrogator was fascinated that Robert mentioned God in his statement.

"We Russians have sent a man into space. We've reached the heavens, but no one was there. How can so many people believe there is a God in heaven when we proved there is none?"

Not being interested in debating theology, Robert suggested politely they change the subject.

"No, really, this fascinates me. Please continue. And, by the way, I like you. We could become good friends."

Sitting in the police station, Robert just shook his head in astonishment.

Robert and Sy spent the night in the Moscow Jail, with crumbling plaster walls and a general state of disrepair that was not unusual in the Russian buildings of that era. The questioning by various interrogators continued throughout the night until Robert and Sy were exhausted.

Neither of them had eaten a morsel since lunch. They didn't have an opportunity to order anything at the Metropole's restaurant before they had been arrested. Robert asked if there was anything to eat, and their interrogators indicated there wasn't at the facility where they were, at least. Perhaps they would be transferred tomorrow to a facility that had food. The idea they would still be in custody the next day did not improve Robert's appetite or his spirits.

"We do not want you to think less of the Russian government. We are indeed sorry there is not food for you here."

Robert considered it interesting that the first time he spoke in a somewhat dispirited fashion, the Russian interrogators were insulted. It seemed they were determined to get him to sign a confession, but on the other hand, they didn't want Robert to think less of them. As interesting as the experience was, Robert didn't want to repeat it ever again.

By the next day, Robert and Sy were both released from the Moscow Jail. Robert received $500 of his money back, but the Minox camera and the remainder of his $974 had disappeared. Robert didn't complain. He was too grateful to be free.

As soon as they were released, the two doctors immediately returned to their hotel room. While they were gone, a new radio had appeared in the room, and they quietly debated as to whether or not this was really a new radio or a listening device. Sy decided to ensure that any listeners would consider them non-threatening to the Russian way of life, and he began to ramble on about what a great country Russia was and how he admired the government. He was his usual funny self, but Robert shushed him. They grabbed their baggage and went straight to the Moscow Airport and took the first plane they could find that would land in a Western country.

Their haven turned out to be Sweden. When they arrived, they reported their adventure to a United States Embassy official in Stockholm. The story of the Russian escapade eventually made its way into American newspapers, though it's uncertain at this time exactly how that occurred. Embassy officials would have preferred a "no comment" from Robert and Sy when they were asked about the incident by the media, but the officials made it clear that the two of them could say anything they wanted to.

Sy and Robert also learned the circumstances surrounding their release. Apparently, two Russians had recently been arrested at the United Nations, and the Russian government attempted to trade two hapless Americans for those two Russians.

That didn't work, but the next day Professor Barghoorn, a professor at Harvard University who also happened to be a friend and former professor of President Kennedy, was arrested in Moscow. The professor was a more valuable pawn for the Russian government, so Robert and Sy were released. Later, President Kennedy threatened to end all cultural exchanges with the USSR if they did not release the professor. After about three weeks, the Russians complied.

Robert wondered what would have happened if the Russians had not chosen the professor to replace the two of them.

Sy telephoned his family at home and decided to fly back to the United States directly from Stockholm. As far as he was concerned, the trip was finished. Robert went on to finish the tour alone.

His next stop had already been planned for East Berlin so it didn't make Robert feel very comfortable or secure to hear the citizens there bragging that they were "the best communists, even better than the Russians." The Russian experience in jail had provided Robert and Sy with more communist experience than they ever wanted.

Robert continued with his trip into East Berlin despite some misgivings and wondered if he was being brave or merely crazy to go behind the iron curtain after the arrest in Moscow. His heart was in his mouth as he went through Checkpoint Charlie. As he waited at the border, he soon realized the guard was not just checking his passport but was looking something up in a logbook or ledger of some kind. Robert wondered if they were aware that he'd recently been in jail in Moscow, and he was concerned that somehow they would use that technicality to impede his travels, or even worse, find an excuse to arrest him.

But the guard approved his passage. The round the world trip would continue, with the remainder being fascinating but uneventful—at least as far as jail time was concerned.

# 8

# HEMA GEL
## PATENT PROBLEMS

ROBERT PLANNED A TRIP TO PRAGUE WITH MARTIN POLLOCK, who was then Vice President of National Patent Development Company. At the time, Robert was under the impression that Pollock would be his lawyer in negotiating the patent rights with Czechoslovakia for the HEMA gel.

Pollock had explained to Robert that National Patent Development Company had experience in representing a number of large companies abroad, and in past dealings he'd learned that the compensation was always paid by the Eastern European country, not by the patent holder, which would be Robert. The deal they intended to make would provide Pollock with compensation from the Czech representatives in the amount of five cents out of each dollar that Robert paid the Czechs in royalties.

Robert was elated. The money could be significant if he could successfully market a new soft contact lens, but the financial gain was almost an afterthought. He wanted to master the challenge. Once the patent rights were assigned to him, he could finally get the actual development underway in order to begin manufacturing and marketing the new soft lens.

They arrived at the Prague legal offices where they would meet the Czech representatives. In front of them was an elevator unlike any that Robert had ever seen before. It consisted of a series of nonstop cubes that were spaced out on a mammoth, belt-like device that shifted from one level to another. The system was basically like a ski resort's chair lift in that people had to step on and off the cubes as they revolved. It never stopped, leading Robert to wonder how, in heaven's name, someone with a handicap could ever get safely on or off.

Professor Wichterle, a representative from the firm Polytechna named Mr. Sronek, and a patent attorney joined Robert and Pollock in the conference room. After the introductions and handshakes, the small group sat around the table and discussed the division of patent rights and royalties.

It was agreed that Robert's royalty contract would cover the rights to market the HEMA gel throughout the Western Hemisphere and a few other countries. Robert would have liked an even greater area, but when he asked Mr. Sronek about adding more countries, the man balked  and commented that the addition of Western Europe would be too large an area for Robert to handle in manufacturing and marketing. They also agreed that if there were any disputes in the future, arbitration would be conducted, not in the U.S. or in Czechoslovakia, but in the neutral country of Sweden.

Overall, the deal pleased Robert. At one point, Robert asked Professor Wichterle if he would make the spin casting machine for them, and the professor answered affirmatively. He could make the machine for $100,000.

Robert inquired, "But if you made two spin casting machines at the same time?"

"Then I could do them both for $150,000."

"Fine, a fair price."

Martin Pollock turned toward Robert with a look on his face that clearly told Robert he was being too easy. Pollock whispered, "Look, you do the science and I will do the negotiations."

Robert replied, "It's a fair price and I don't want to spoil our nice relationship with offers, counteroffers, and complex negotiations."

It was agreed upon. The contract would be drawn up, and the participants would reconvene in the same location in a few days to hold a signing ceremony.

A few days later, Robert passed through the strange elevator system and returned to the conference room where he was to sign the final contract. As he reviewed the contract, he noticed one important detail was very different than what had been agreed upon.

The deal the Czechs were making for the HEMA patent rights listed *not* Robert Morrison, but a company called Flexible Contact Lens Company with guarantees by the National Patent Development Company and by Robert.

"Just a minute. There's a mistake here. The contract should be between me and the Czechoslovakia Academy of Science. I never heard of the Flexible Contact Lens Company."

"Dr. Morrison, we have met with Mr. Pollock. He says you will own half of the Flexible Contact Lens Company."

"I've never even heard of that company before." Robert was confused. This had to be a mistake, but a little voice somewhere deep in his brain nagged at him: *You're being screwed.* He didn't want to believe it. "You must remove that name and put in mine."

"The Flexible Contact Lens Company is incorporated in Delaware. Mr. Pollock and Mr. Gerald Feldman filed the paperwork just before leaving the United States to come here. Perhaps they just neglected to tell you."

Now it seemed clear to Robert that Pollock and Feldman were working against him. Pollock had met with the Czech representatives without Robert's knowledge in the intervening days since the last joint meeting.

"The contract must be in my name."

"Actually, Dr. Morrison, Mr. Pollock made a good point yesterday," said Sronek. "He mentioned that it would be in our best interests to have not just one, but two guarantors of the contract. We do like that idea."

The contract would provide the Czechs with one dollar per lens, a minimum of $100,000 per year after FDA approval of the HEMA material's use in soft contact lenses, and it allowed the lenses to be sold in the United States.

"No way," Robert gestured toward Pollock. "This man was representing me as my patent attorney. It's against the law in the United States for a lawyer to move in on a client without agreement."

"We're not in the United States," Pollock pointed out.

Sronek interjected a comment that Robert saw as a serious threat. "Dr. Morrison, you must take your half or none. We are dealing with Mr. Pollock."

Robert didn't know how to respond. This development was unexpected, and the treachery was a kick to his gut. The anger and betrayal coursed through him, and it was difficult for him to think straight. The lawyer he thought he had working for him, wasn't. He was alone, dealing with a situation that he didn't know how to handle.

Robert was not a lawyer and he didn't have one now. If he didn't sign, he might lose everything he'd worked for so far. He decided to sign. The contract was between the Czechs and the Flexible Contact Lens Company, guaranteed by the National Patent Development Company and Dr. Robert Morrison.

Later, Robert paced through the Prague streets. How had it come to this? All the work, the dreams, the plans he had—seemed to have turned as gray as the cool soot on the city's buildings. In one fell swoop, Pollock and his crew had somehow wrested the patent away from him.

He wondered if Pollock had provided a bribe of some sort—gifts, watches, money? He didn't know. He just knew that he was livid, and that was an emotion that was rare to Robert. He, who had told his family he never even wanted to say the word *hate*. They'd even teased him when he insisted the children had to spell the word out if they ever used it—H-A-T-E.

Right now, he could spell it easily in his own fast-paced walk, and he had a strong urge to punch someone. Pollock and Feldman were first on the list.

He walked up and down the cobblestone streets in such a turmoil, he didn't even notice where he was going. He was powerless.

With a black cloud enveloping him, Robert conceded defeat. He consoled himself with the rationalization that half was better than none.

Ruth met Robert when he arrived back at the New York airport, along with their housekeeper, Mary Matthews. More surprising, Gerald Feldman was standing just behind the two ladies.

Feldman was the last person Robert wanted to see at that moment. He'd showed up at the airport in a particularly good mood because Pollock had phoned him explaining that Robert was great at the meeting and had asked the Czechs not to pay royalties until the FDA approved the product.

"Dr. Morrison, congratulations. Martin is extremely happy to be working with you, and we're now partners."

One sentence passed through Robert's mind: *They are crooked as a barrel of snakes!* Robert couldn't control himself any longer. He grabbed a handful of the front of Feldman's shirt and tie in a tight fist, a fist that would have been on the guy's jaw if he'd let go of the fabric.

"Listen, Feldman. You and Pollock are the lawyers. I am not. But I want something right now that says I own half of the Flexible Contact Lens Company."

"Let go of me!" Feldman pulled away. "Let go and I'll give you your paperwork." Feldman happened to be holding a paperback book, and he simply tore off the back cover and asked, "Anyone have a pen?"

Ruth searched her purse and handed one over.

Feldman scratched out the words on the paperback cover: "This is to certify that Robert Morrison owns half of the Flexible Contact Lens Company." Then he signed it: "Gerald Feldman, President, National Patent Development Company." Robert had Mary Matthews sign as a witness.

Robert knew he needed professional legal help to ensure that even the half share of the Flexible Contact Lens Company didn't somehow disappear. He'd already made multiple calls to Martin Pollock asking for a 50 percent share of the company with no result.

Robert hired Francis B. Haas, Jr., a lawyer and childhood friend who now worked at the legal firm of McNees, Wallace, and Nurick. The two set up a meeting in New York City during which Pollock said that the Flexible Contact Lens Company would give Robert Morrison a third, not a half share. Allen Isen would receive a percentage of the company as well, but the National Patent Development Company would gain control.

Robert was brief and to the point. "I expect half or I am leaving."

"Dr. Morrison, we are offering you a third. That is the deal now."

"If I leave here, I will do what I have to do to enforce our agreement, which was for half."

"At this point, a third share is all we can provide."

Robert turned to Frank Haas and choked out the words, "Let's go!"

He picked up his briefcase. As they walked out the door onto Park Avenue, he turned to Haas. "I want to hire the biggest and best law firm in America and sue."

Frank Haas immediately arranged for Robert to meet with Jim

Purcell, an attorney with the legal group of Paul, Weiss, Rifkind. The attorney, Rifkind, was well-connected. He had been a federal judge and also a friend and advisor to FDR when he was in the White House.

Attorney Jim Purcell listened carefully to the tale, from Robert's first meeting with Professor Wichterle, to the unexpected creation of the National Patent Development Company which took over half of Robert's patent rights, to the meeting in New York where that half was reduced to a third. Robert told Mr. Purcell about grabbing Gerald Feldman's shirt, worried that he might be charged with assault. Purcell said it was great, and he was glad Robert had done it. He should not be concerned at all.

When the reconstruction of events had ended, Jim Purcell sat back and announced that they should definitely sue.

"The good news is you have that book cover. It's signed by Gerald Feldman, giving you a half share, and that's the only proof you have."

Robert blessed his impulse that day at the airport when he'd insisted Feldman sign something.

They decided to immediately serve Martin Pollock with notice of the suit. In total, they would sue Martin Pollock, Gerald Feldman, the National Patent Development Company, and Allen Isen.

"It won't be easy to get Martin Pollock to accept delivery," Robert told Purcell. "I'm sure the secretary will simply say he's out, even if he's in the next room."

"I appreciate the tip, Robert, but we've had this problem before. I'll get an expert to handle it." Purcell smiled. He used the intercom to call a lawyer who, he explained, was currently clerking for the law firm.

A young woman appeared in the doorway, and Purcell explained what he wanted her to do.

"She's rather comely," Purcell said with a wink. *Comely* was an old-fashioned term, but Robert agreed that it fit the young law-yer. He was beginning to see Purcell's method and liked the idea.

He later learned that the young woman had visited the National Patent Development Company offices and very sweetly had asked, "Is Martin here?"

The secretary looked over the shapely, young woman. "Who wants him?"

The young woman smiled confidently. "I'm a friend of his."

Martin Pollock came out to the reception area, pushing up his necktie. He greeted the young woman with a big smile on his face. "Hello, young lady. What can I do for you?"

The young lawyer thrust the paperwork into Pollock's out-stretched hand. "You're served."

She immediately returned to Purcell's office and explained that the mission had been successfully accomplished. Purcell laughed heartily. The ploy had worked once again.

While she'd been gone, Purcell introduced Robert to Jay Top-kiss, who would be the litigator if the case could not be settled and they had to go to court. Robert remembered Martin Pollock once telling him that he'd rather sue someone than have a product because settlements can be far more lucrative than actually having something to sell. A settlement was obviously possible but so was the potential for having to go to court.

As Robert was leaving the offices, Purcell commented that a good lawyer takes care of himself first. He asked Robert to leave a check for $5,000. It was the first of several in the legal battle that would stretch out for years.

The lawsuit was for a total of $60 million, which included defendants Pollock, Feldman, the National Patent Development Company, and Isen for $15 million each. The suit was filed in the Federal Court of New York.

Pollock's National Patent Development Company had hired Strook, Strook & Levan, a law firm that was well-known in the area. The latter requested a settlement meeting with Robert and Jim Purcell.

Jim and Robert agreed to the meeting, and during the discussion, the National Patent Development Company offered to buy Robert out on the basis of a half share. The idea of a third had been dropped by the wayside, thanks to the cover of the paperback book that Feldman had signed acknowledging Robert's half share.

Robert countered by offering to buy *their* half share.

In the end, they simply tossed a coin and Robert lost. The deal eventually agreed upon was that the National Patent Development Company would buy Robert out by paying a sum each month for the next ten years. If they missed even one payment, then by three in the afternoon on the last day of the month, all the patent rights would revert to Robert.

"Don't worry, Bob," said Purcell. "I've checked them out, and they have no money. They might find an Uncle Louie who will help them for a month, maybe someone else for a second month, but it will all be yours very soon. They can't make the payments."

"I don't like this deal at all. They may find a bank or someone to finance this."

"No use in being greedy. Trust me. I know what I'm doing and greed is not attractive."

Robert felt a twinge of guilt. He hated even the appearance of greed, but the deal concerned him and he tried again.

"If this fails, why not at least get me an exclusive in Pennsylvania."

Purcell sighed as though speaking to a child. "You don't have to be selfish. In any case, don't worry. It will soon be completely yours."

The payment schedule began. Some months the payments arrived for deposit in Robert's account at Dauphin Deposit Trust Company with only minutes left before the National Patent Development Company was to lose the rights. Each month Robert checked with the bank. Each time the clock ticked closer to three without a check, he'd hold his breath. Five minutes ... and it would be his.

But each month the check struggled in. This continued for six months.

Then Robert learned that the optical company, Bausch & Lomb, had borrowed the money to pay Robert's contract off completely. The lawyers representing Robert apologized to their client, never dreaming Bausch & Lomb would be able to swing the deal. Though Bausch & Lomb was the second largest optical company after American Optical at the time, the company had been closing down some operations, and it appeared that it was about to go under. Instead, they managed to get bank financing to pay off the contract.

Robert was out, but his patent rights helped Bausch & Lomb to thrive. Eventually, the company would capture billions of dollars worth of business in lenses and lens solutions.

It was later estimated that the payment Bausch & Lomb had made to Robert was worth more than $100 million in lost royalties. After that, Robert continued to follow the progress of the HEMA gel as developed by National Patent Development Company. He noted the company would periodically issue press releases on a new potential use for the HEMA gel material. Robert recalled those uses ranged from filters in cigarettes to a washable paint for bridges and walls to a liner for dentures. The company's stock advanced each time.

A few years later, while Robert was walking down the sidewalk on Madison Avenue in New York, he happened to see Martin Pollock. The first thing Pollock asked him was "Are you wired?"

Robert looked down at his light summer shirt and chino pants and wondered how Pollock could even think he might be wearing a tape recorder. More importantly, what difference would it make anyway?

When Pollock was assured that Robert wasn't taping the conversation for any future legal action, he said, "I've always wanted to thank you."

"Thank me?" That was the last thing Robert expected to hear.

"We made lots of money on that HEMA deal thanks to you. I couldn't put that into writing, of course."

"I imagine not."

"Well, I just always wanted to say thank-you." And Martin Pollock walked away.

## 9

---

### THE FIRST ROYAL PATIENT

T HE PHONE RANG AT SIX THAT EVENING. AS USUAL, ROBERT WAS still in the office since he normally worked until at least seven, sometimes as late as ten. When he answered, the caller introduced himself as being the private physician to His Majesty King Baudouin of Belgium.

Robert laughed. His first thought was his boyhood friend Charley Grubmeyer was calling. Charley always enjoyed a good practical joke, but the person on the other end of the line seemed to have an authentic French accent, and he said he was a special representative of the king of Belgium. The fact that his call could be legitimate hit Robert as suddenly and unexpectedly as a winning lottery number.

His Majesty King Baudouin of Belgium was requesting that Dr. Robert Morrison make a house call to the Royal Palace in Brussels. Dr. Morrison had been referred to the king by a doctor in Brussels, a member of the Belgian Ophthalmological Society who had heard Robert speak at one of the group's meetings.

In several tries, the Belgian doctor had failed to improve the king's vision sufficiently. King Baudouin had a total of five pairs of contact lenses from five different doctors from five different countries. All were comfortable to wear, and the king had a special favorite in a pair that had been imported from Germany, but his vision was still bothersome.

The very next day Robert flew to Brussels as a guest of the Belgian airline, Sabena. He didn't even pass through customs but was immediately whisked through the airport to the Brussels Hilton.

That afternoon a private car picked him up at the hotel and delivered him to the Royal Palace in Laeken about twenty miles from Brussels. The palace was the height of elegance by any world standard, but it was the gardens for which the palace was famous. The grounds required one hundred gardeners to tend to the shrubs and plants, trees, lawn, and flowers. Even orange trees were in bloom. Robert noted that these were planted in dark green boxes in greenhouses with controlled heat and humidity. Another greenhouse held colorful azaleas and still another held a variety of exotic tropical plants.

Statues and copies of famous structures around the world dotted the grounds, including a copy of the Greek Acropolis. A pond held two rare black swans, a gift from another European royal.

King Baudouin and Queen Fabiola were as formal as their home, with a regal and tranquil dignity. Despite the formality, each was extremely gracious and polite to their visiting eye doctor.

The morning of the eye exam, an aide showed Robert to an elegantly appointed room with lush draperies, gold framed artwork, and plush furnishings. It wasn't a proper clinical setting at all, but Robert had brought the essential equipment with him. He would improvise on this eye exam. Later, they were to drive to a doctor's office in Brussels where Robert could borrow a slit lamp to view the eye microscopically and measure the intraocular pressure to help determine the possible presence of glaucoma.

He glanced around the room. It contained lovely antique furniture and thick rugs on polished wood floors. The walls were hung with oil paintings, most of them portraits. One was a large portrait

# SOME FRIENDS, PATIENTS,
# AND TENNIS ACQUAINTANCES
# OF DR. ROBERT MORRISON

Dr. Morrison and the Rolls-Royce from the Queen of Holland

Robert and His Majesty King Baudouin of Belgium

His Serene Highness Prince Albert of Monaco and Robert playing tennis at the Morrison house in Harrisburg

HSH Prince Albert, Ruth, and Robert at Robert's Park Avenue office

Robert's daughter, Patty Morrison Schimberg, being kissed by HSH Prince Albert and Andre St. Mleux, Prince Albert's best friend and renowned financial advisor

HSH Prince Albert and Robert

HSH Prince Albert, Patty, and Robert

His Royal Highness
Prince Bernhard in
front of the Royal
Palace in Soesdijk,
Holland

HRH Prince Bernhard,
the prince of the Netherlands

Her Royal Highness
Princess Christina
of the Netherlands
in yellow; Nora,
Lady-in-Waiting,
in blue

Robert and Ruth with
Princess Antoinette of
Monaco, sister to the
late Prince Rainier

HRH Prince Bernhard congratulating Dr. Morrison

HRH Prince Bernhard
and Robert at
the Knighting Ceremony

Robert being
knighted

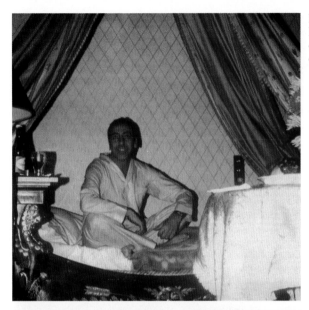

Robert at the Royal
Palace in Belgium
on a bed Napoleon
once slept in

Princess Paula Al Sabah of Kuwait with Robert

Her Majesty Queen
Juliana of Holland
next to Robert
in front of the
Royal Palace

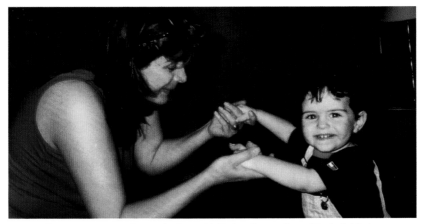

Princess Sarvenaz of Iran playing with Robert's grandson. Hugh Schimberg

Dick Thornburgh,
then governor
of Pennsylvania

(left to right) Richard Zimmerman, CEO, Chairman of the Board of Hershey Foods; Edward Rosen, CEO, Chairman of the Board of Raymond Rosen and Company and renowned philanthropist; George Blankenship, M.D., President of the American Academy of Ophthalmology and Chairman of the Department of Ophthalmology at Penn State University College of Medicine; Richard Thornburgh, then Attorney General of the United States

Richard Thornburgh,
Ruthie, and Robert

Robert with Adnan Khashoggi and his wife in London; Khashoggi was, at the time,
reported to be the richest man in the world

Robert and
Regis Philbin

Mike Douglas and his wife with Robert. Robert was on Douglas' TV show twice

Roger Moore with Robert

Robert and Ruth (middle) with movie star Elkie Somers on the far left and tennis great Monica Seles on the far right

"Love Boat" doctor
Bernie Koppel
with Robert

Movie star
Robert Loggia
and Robert

Sean Connery
and Dr. Morrison

Chuck Norris and Robert

Wonder Woman,
Lynda Carter,
who made many
visits to Harrisburg

Sean Connery with
the Morrisons

Neil Simon with Robert on the tennis court

Robert and Ruthie
with Neil Simon
and his wife Diane

Lloyd Bridges and Robert

L.A. Dodgers great
Steve Garvey along
with Dr. Morrison

Sharon Stone
and Robert

Bill Cosby and Robert

Mary Fran,
Bob Newhart's wife
on "Newhart"
TV show
with Robert

TV and movie stars Alan Thicke and Joanna Kerns with the Morrisons

Movie star Robert Stack with Dr. Morrison

(left to right) Fred Stolle, tennis great who won
Wimbledon and U.S. Open Doubles Titles; TV and
movie star Richard Anderson; and the Morrisons

Robert with
Eric Braeden, star of
the soap "The Young
and the Restless"

Supermodel
Cheryl Tieg,
who interviewed
Robert on
"Good Morning
America"

NBA Coach
Pat Riley with
the Morrisons

Wayne Rogers of "MASH" fame with his wife and the Morrisons

Kathy Lee Gifford with the Morrisons

of a distinguished man; it was labeled *King Leopold*. Robert imagined he was the king's father or grandfather.

He didn't spend too much time admiring the art, however. That particular frame happened to be well-placed for his needs and it even had a space on the bottom of the frame between the wood and the regal portrait. Robert tucked the Snellen eye chart into that frame.

The king chuckled. "I see we have finally put that portrait to good use!"

Robert asked the king to read the eye chart. In excellent English, spoken with a slight French accent, he read the letters from the top down. He managed to read them correctly until he reached the line that would indicate his eyesight was 20/40. A normal reading of 20/20 vision means the person sees at 20 feet exactly what the eye should see at 20 feet. The king saw it as though it were 40 feet away.

Robert used the retinoscope he'd brought in order to determine the exact refractive error. He noted the astigmatism was about one diopter in the right eye and one-and-a-quarter diopter in the left eye. He determined that King Baudouin had astigmatism. Based on the king's current prescription, apparently every other eye doctor who had examined him had either not found it or simply ignored it.

Robert reached into his bag and got the astigmatic test lens, positioning it properly in front of the German lens that was already on the king's eye. He asked him to read the eye chart again. This time King Baudouin was able to read the chart with the results at a normal 20/20.

"This is wonderful. I can read it easily ... so amazing!" Robert turned the lens 90 degrees and everything blurred once more. Then he realigned the lens to the proper position and the king smiled broadly.

"Your Majesty, I'll send you a pair of contact lenses that will be slightly weighted so they will stay positioned properly on your eyes, and you should be able to read very well."

Robert admitted later that, in his opinion, he did nothing great. "I merely corrected his vision as it should have been done by the five doctors that preceded me."

He was also modest enough to comment "if any of them had done good work, King Baudouin would never have invited me to consult with him." And that, as Robert readily admits, would have been a shame, because that experience with King Baudouin was to be the beginning of an almost fairy tale existence.

THOSE WERE THE DAYS OF RIGID LENSES. ROBERT CONTINUED TO visit King Baudouin every year, sometimes twice a year, for 22 years. Usually Robert stayed at the Brussels Hilton, and it soon became a routine for His Majesty's aide-de-camp, an Army colonel, to meet Robert at the hotel and escort him personally to the palace.

Each time the chauffeur-driven limousine pulled up to the awesome palace, the colonel guided Robert to the same lovely room in order to chat for awhile as they were waiting to see the king. On each visit, the colonel always asked Robert about the weather in the United States. Robert would tell him, then Robert would ask the colonel about the weather in Belgium and the colonel would respond. Eventually, Robert called the room the Weather Room in front of King Baudouin who looked puzzled until Robert explained how every single visit was preceded by a chat about the weather in that same room.

King Baudouin laughed heartily at the explanation, and from that moment on, he could joke about the Weather Room. The two men became good friends, and Robert shared family dinners with the king and the queen, joined by Ruthie when she accompanied Robert on his trips, and sometimes the children.

The lack of children had been painful for the royal couple. Queen Fabiola had suffered miscarriages. At the time, Robert wasn't sure how to approach the topic. In the interest of helping the couple who had become his good friends, he broached the sensitive topic one day and asked the queen if she would like him to bring an American professor who specialized in such problems. She told him no, that such things were God's will, and if He willed her to have a child, she would. If not, then she would accept that.

During the course of their friendship, King Baudouin was generous with gifts, and since he was a great supporter of the arts, many gifts he offered Robert were art books that he and the queen would autograph. King Baudouin was especially proud of the famous Belgian artist Bruegel, so Robert received a large tabletop volume called *Our Bruegel*, which today sits in a prominent place on the shelf in his retirement condo in Florida.

The king displayed a grand oil painting which hung in the palace, the most famous piece he owned, a painting of the Tower of Babel. One time he produced a magnifying glass and held it out to Robert, explaining how it would show the finest of details, including tiny mustaches of the numerous people in the painting. It also showed clergymen giving orders to slaves who were building the tower.

The king and his wife were strict Catholics. Robert remembers being told that Queen Fabiola had once planned to be a nun, but gave up the idea to be queen. She was from Spain.

At one dinner shared with Robert's entire family—Ruthie, Patty, and Jim—the queen told of two close family members who had taken the oath of silence and slept on boards all their lives. Robert could tell how much she admired them for their unusual devotion. Patty, who was just ten years old, said, "I really don't understand that at all, but I do admire their devotion and strong beliefs."

Robert looked at his child and gaped in awe. Surely, this life that included visiting royal palaces had produced an amazingly tactful child.

During one of his Brussels visits, Robert was sitting in a restaurant near the palace, trying to read the paper in French. Suddenly, four words popped out at him: *Robert, Morrison, Harrisburg,* and *America*. His faulty French translated enough to understand "fit contact lens and it cost $20 million."

Twenty million dollars! He didn't think he was being paid anything close to that, but Robert entertained himself for a few moments, imagining the wonderful things he could do with $20 million.

He motioned the waiter over to order a refill on his coffee.

"Waiter, can you speak English? Can you explain this to me?"

The waiter read the article and enlightened Robert to the fact that he shouldn't start spending the $20 million. The Belgian treasury would be doing that.

Since King Baudouin was now successfully wearing contact lenses to improve his vision without glasses, he wanted all the official portraits redone to show himself as the handsome man he was—without glasses. The money mentioned in the article referred to the cost to reprint postage stamps, currency, and coins in his realm.

Robert's visits to the palace in Belgium continued until the king died of prostate cancer at the age of 62. Since he had no children to inherit the Belgian throne, King Baudouin's younger brother, Albert, became king.

The last gifts that King Baudouin sent to Robert were a handsome pair of gold cuff links with the king's official seal plus a silver tray engraved "To Dr. and Mrs. Robert Jay Morrison, Brussels, July 14, 1974." The engraving held the signatures of King Baudouin and Queen Fabiola.

When Robert and Ruth tried to telephone the palace to thank

King Baudouin personally, they learned of his death. Robert still feels badly that he was never able to talk to him again or to thank him for that last thoughtful gift.

# 10

## THE ROYAL GRAPEVINE

T HE CLERK SLID A TELEPHONE MEMO ACROSS THE HOTEL'S FRONT desk, looking at Robert with new respect in his eyes. Robert picked up the small piece of paper and read the neat script in ballpoint pen. The message could have been any of the thousands of mundane messages that anyone receives throughout the years from friends, family, coworkers, neighbors, or bosses. This message, however, noted that Queen Juliana of the Netherlands had called.

Below the impressive name was a long series of numbers which the clerk explained was the telephone number for the Royal Palace in the Netherlands, including the correct country code. Monsieur could dial the number in privacy from his room. Unspoken, of course, was the fact that the desk clerk was extremely curious to know why this rather unassuming and seemingly unexceptional American man would be receiving a message from the queen of the Netherlands. Actually, so did the American himself.

Robert placed the call from his room. A receptionist responded and put him on hold for what seemed like a long time but was probably just a few minutes. Then a female voice answered. He expected it to be the receptionist again or perhaps a personal secretary to the queen. It was Queen Juliana herself. In a strong voice that was firm and kind, she explained why she had called him.

"Dr. Morrison, you have been highly recommended by King Baudouin. He suggested I contact you immediately for an appointment before you return to the United States."

Robert had inadvertently discovered the royal grapevine.

"How can I help you, um ..." He paused, not sure how to address the queen of the Netherlands, finally settling for "Your Majesty."

"We would appreciate it if you could find time to visit us here. We would like to consult you on some eye problems." The queen was obviously reluctant to go into personal details on the telephone.

"If you can oblige us, I can make flight arrangements for tomorrow and send a car to meet you at the airport here."

Robert thought quickly, mentally processing the possibilities. The Netherlands was a hop, skip, and a jump from Brussels. He could easily fit in the appointment in the neighboring country ... another kingdom heard from, so to speak.

King Baudouin had arranged to help his friend, the queen of the Netherlands. Early the next morning, one of his royal limousines arrived to pick up Robert at the hotel and take him to the Brussels Airport. Robert boarded a commercial flight to Amsterdam where he was welcomed by another limousine, this one belonging to Queen Juliana.

What had at first been an entirely new experience in being treated like royalty was fast becoming a habit. On the second limo ride, Robert considered the fact that he could easily learn to enjoy being pampered like this.

When he checked in at the Amstel Hotel, the desk clerk provided another message from Queen Juliana. He was to have a good evening, and her limousine would pick him up the next morning to take him to the palace for the appointment with the queen and her family.

THE LIMOUSINE MOVED THROUGH AMSTERDAM'S MID-MORNING traffic. As the vehicle pulled up to stoplights, Robert began to notice the pedestrians waiting to cross the street, wanting to get a good look into the limousine's windows. Those were the days before tinted window glass so the pedestrians could see the occupants clearly. They fully expected to see either Queen Juliana or Prince Bernhard in the backseat. Instead, there was Robert.

He hated to disappoint the citizens who thought they would catch a glimpse of the royal family, so each time the limousine stopped and someone on the sidewalk appeared to be looking toward him, he tried to give a regal nod. Perhaps they'd think they had seen another visiting royal and not an optometrist from Harrisburg, Pennsylvania.

On the drive, the chauffeur explained that the royal family did not normally live in the formal Royal Palace in the center of Amsterdam. The palace was used for entertaining and official functions. He was now driving Robert to the family's actual residence, about 25 miles outside the city. It was a much more casual home.

Soestdijk Palace appeared anything but casual to Robert's eyes. As they approached the gate, a guard snapped to attention and saluted. The chauffeur drove them through, and they traveled the equivalent of a few city blocks between the gate and the palace, past beautifully manicured grounds punctuated by majestic trees and flowering plants.

Soestdijk Palace consisted of a central, two-story, white structure with two wings. The palace was originally built as a royal hunting lodge in the seventeenth century. Later it was seized during Napoleon's invasion and became an inn for French troops. Eventually, the palace was given to William II of the Netherlands because of his efforts leading the combined Dutch and Belgian forces at the Battle of Waterloo. Queen Juliana and Prince Bernhard lived in Soestdijk Palace for more than 60 years.

An escort showed Robert to a guest suite on the first floor

of the palace, in the right hand wing. As soon as Robert entered the suite, he noticed the wallpaper and bedspreads were done in a matching blue print; everything in the suite, in fact, seemed to match.

During subsequent visits, when Robert and Ruth brought their children, the prince had given the wide-eyed Jim and Patty a tour of the entire palace, with Robert and Ruth trailing along behind. Robert noticed that the queen's bedroom was twice the size of Prince Bernhard's.

Prince Bernhard was a charming fellow, slightly raffish, but handsomely groomed. He preferred light blue, button down collar shirts and wore a carnation in his lapel. Where the carnation habit began, Robert didn't know, but he soon learned that even when Prince Bernhard traveled, an aide made sure a fresh carnation would be delivered to his hotel room each day.

Eventually, Robert and Prince Bernhard were to become close friends. Whenever Robert was visiting the Netherlands, they'd sit in Bernhard's office, cluttered with his collection of elephant figurines of all sizes, made of ivory, jade, and wood. They'd chat about everything from politics to golf, family to history, especially focusing on World War II.

The prince had been born into German nobility, but he had gained respect from the Dutch when he worked with the resistance against Hitler. During the early German invasion, he was said to have grabbed a machine gun and organized the Palace Guards to repel German paratroopers.

The Nazi occupation had forced his wife, then Princess Juliana, and their two daughters, Beatrix and Irene, to flee, first to London, then to Canada for the duration of the war. Prince Bernhard joined the resistance in England and served as a pilot for the Allies in the Royal Air Force. After the war the monarchs returned to help rebuild their country that had been devastated by the German invasion.

Robert and Prince Bernhard developed a rare friendship, perhaps because each was not only intelligent and independent in spirit but irrepressible. As a young man, the prince had shown his dashing personality by arriving for his first official visit to his fiancée, the then Crown Princess Juliana, in a powerful car. He raced into the town until stopped by a policeman, who actually apologized to the prince, but requested the young man please slow down while in the country.

Despite the trappings of royalty and the rumors of immense wealth, Queen Juliana and Prince Bernhard were heads of a warm, loving family. Robert could even believe the story passed throughout the world, which he knew could have been an exaggeration but sounded like something the gracious queen might do.

As the story goes, the queen invited some of her country's farm women to the Royal Palace for an event promoting agriculture. Having never dined in any setting more elegant than a cafe, one of the farm women mistakenly picked up a finger bowl, with its neat slice of lemon floating in it, and drank the water. Perhaps she'd thought it was some form of lemonade. In any case, to avoid embarrassing the woman, the queen picked up her own finger bowl and drank it as well.

The family had four daughters: Beatrix, who later became queen; Irene, who married the prince of Spain; Margriet; and the last born, Princess Marijke Christina.

It was Princess Christina, the baby of the family and a young adult at the time, who needed attention. It had become rumored that Princess Christina was virtually blind. It was also understood by Robert that treating the royals meant discretion. In all his years treating royalty and celebrities, Robert kept their problems to himself. He could never confirm or deny that he was their eye doctor unless they first mentioned it in public. Further, he would never discuss what his services entailed, what the specific eye problem or diagnosis was, or even admit that the person wore contact lenses. His code of silence lasted decades.

However, various magazines at the time had reported Princess Christina had very limited vision, and Dr. Morrison would never comment on such matters. The eye problems were thought to have originated when her mother contracted rubella when she was pregnant with her. Though Christina loved to sing and play the piano, she could hardly read music.

Robert performed a standard eye examination, and it was quickly evident that Princess Christina's eye problem was grave. She couldn't read even the very largest, top line of the eye chart. At the time, the various international news magazines, including *Newsweek* and *Time,* were investigating whether or not the princess had an artificial eye. Later, a reporter from *Time* called Robert and corralled him with a direct question, "Does she or doesn't she?" Only Robert knew for sure and he wasn't talking.

His response was one he'd learned to provide any news service over the decades of working with celebrities. "I'm not at liberty to say. I'll neither confirm nor deny." Just to be polite and avoid slamming the phone down, Dr. Morrison always added, "I am going to wish you good luck in your work and hang up the phone now." Which he did. Nora, the lady-in-waiting for Princess Christina, loved that response.


Robert THOUGHT HE COULD IMPROVE Princess Christina's VISION by taking advantage of the pinhole effect that would possibly help her eye fixate on the objects she viewed such as her music.

The idea that a pinhole could help the eye was not new. A company in South Africa made and sold pinhole eye glasses. Robert, however, decided to make a pinhole contact lens in which the pupillary part of the lens was black with a clear pinhole opening. This unique solution improved on eyeglasses because, unlike glasses, a contact lens would move as the eye moved. Thus, it would focus properly.

He would have to treat the princess in Harrisburg in order to create the contact lens. Queen Juliana and Prince Bernhard balked at the idea of sending their youngest daughter to Harrisburg. They wanted Robert to do the work at the palace or at least in an eye doctor's office in the Netherlands. But Robert's equipment for the relatively new contact lens technology, and especially for the unique pinhole design he intended to use, was all in the states.

Even if he transferred his equipment to the Netherlands, it all operated on the U.S. 110 volt system. It wouldn't work on European power that operated on 210 or 220 volts. He could use a converter, but he couldn't be sure that there wouldn't be any problems. No, it made sense to have Princess Christina come to him in Harrisburg where he felt comfortable with the equipment and could ensure the best results.


Princess Christina arrived in Harrisburg with an entourage of three: her lady-in-waiting, Nora, plus two burly bodyguards whose job it was to protect the royal princess from a possible kidnapping attempt.

The princess stayed in Robert's daughter's room, while the bodyguards patrolled the house, alternating shifts throughout the night. Though Robert told them not to worry, they stated that Her Majesty had requested it, and they would not disobey Her Majesty's wishes.

With their approval, however, the Morrisons held two parties to welcome the princess to Harrisburg. One was held just for young adults so she could meet others her own age. The other event was a formal party for which Robert hired Peter Duchin's Orchestra, which had played at the White House.

Robert and Ruth also arranged to take the princess to Philadelphia one evening so she could listen to the Philadelphia Symphony

Orchestra. Another day they traveled to Washington, D.C., where they were able to meet personnel at the Netherlands Embassy.

From the comments Princess Christina later wrote in the Morrisons' guest book, it was obvious she had a good time. She wrote:

> *To kind Bob and Ruth,*
> *I'm going to tell the truth.*
> *My stay I will never forget,*
> *Though I hardly saw my bed.*
> *You did wonderful things for me,*
> *Thankful I will always be.*
> *I can read music and book,*
> *Thanks for all the trouble you took.*

The procedure Robert had planned for Princess Christina was one that worked well for some, but not so well for others. He created the contact lens and fitted it on the princess. He held his breath as she read the eye chart. She could see half of it, which effectively doubled her vision. Christina now could manage to read music and play the piano, an activity that gave her great joy.

Her mother was not only queen of Netherlands with all the power and wealth that that implied, but she was also a member of a royal family that was reputed to be one of the richest in the world. However, Robert didn't request any money for his extraordinary efforts. The Rolls-Royce, delivered to him later in the United States, was Queen Juliana's version of a simple thank-you gift.

Robert never intended for the story about the queen, the princess, and the Rolls-Royce to become public knowledge. A gentleman who'd received a Bentley automobile from the queen mentioned the Rolls-Royce when he was telling his own story to *The Philadelphia Inquirer*. The story was picked up by the Associated Press.

## 11

# THE ROYAL GRAPEVINE
# IN HIGH GEAR

THE MEETINGS WITH KING BAUDOUIN AND QUEEN JULIANA HAD set more than just the wheels of a Rolls-Royce in motion. The royal grapevine went into high gear, recommending Dr. Morrison from one royal family to another, from Europe to the Middle East.

Robert was requested to treat Prince Rainier of Monaco and his wife, Princess Grace, the former Grace Kelly, as well as their son, Prince Albert. On one visit to the Royal Palace in Monaco, Robert was amazed to see Grace Kelly's Oscar sitting casually on a side table in the family's living area.

Often, Ruth and the children would accompany Robert on his treks to Monaco. When Prince Albert was first trying to adjust to his contact lenses, it was 12-year-old Patty who cheerfully taught the 15-year-old prince the trick of inserting the lenses and removing them.

One of the best perks for Robert was a week-long pro-celebrity tournament held each year in Monaco. The tournament was scheduled to begin immediately after The Wimbledon Championships in order to entice the world's top tennis professionals to attend while they were still nearby. Hollywood's brightest stars were flown first class from California and lavished with luxurious accommodations, gourmet meals, and fine wines all provided by the sponsoring companies including Reebok, Volvo, and Alberto Culver.

Robert didn't consider himself in their class, but he was offered the full package and happily mingled with the stars at parties, lunches, banquets, and during the countless rounds of tennis that were played in the stadium at the posh Monaco Country Club.

Robert loved the chance to play his best game. During the years he participated, he won the tournament twice in doubles, once when his partner was Don Budge, one of the greatest tennis players in the world, having won Wimbledon, the U.S. Open, the French, and the Australian Championships. The second time Robert won, his partner was Fred Stolle, who had won doubles at Wimbledon.

Each celebrity, win or lose, received a tennis bag filled with gifts that included monogrammed tee shirts and even tennis shoes, sized correctly. When Robert made the tournament final, he was given several additional tennis outfits, Reebok tennis shoes, and a Prince racket. Since the final was televised, he was requested to use the items to highlight the event's sponsors.

The Monaco Royal Family, of course, was an important part of the event. Two of Prince Rainier and Princess Grace's children, Prince Albert and Princess Caroline, participated in the tennis.

Robert met many celebrities during his stay, including Sharon Stone, Sean Connery, Lloyd Bridges, Lynda Carter (who was then playing Wonder Woman), and Regis Philbin and the producer of his show, Michael Gelman. Not all the stars were Robert's patients, but some became patients after meeting him in Monaco, including Lloyd Bridges. Mr. Bridges later invited Robert to California where Robert examined his eyes.

ONE TIME PRINCE ALBERT WAS VISITING THE MORRISONS AT THEIR home in Harrisburg. They were all invited to the Governor's Mansion for dinner. While they were there, Governor Thornburgh asked Prince Albert what he'd done that day. Prince Albert mentioned that he and Robert had played tennis. The governor asked who'd won and Prince Albert admitted that Robert had, but it was just a warm-up match. Prince Albert laughed and said that he'd get Robert the next day.

The next day they couldn't play on the court at the Morrisons' home because a company from Baltimore had come to put up a tent on the tennis court, so Prince Albert and Robert had to play at the Blue Ridge Country Club. The two men did, and a crowd quickly amassed. Someone even phoned the press; one of the reporters was from the local newspaper and another was from *USA Today*.

While warming up, Prince Albert said with a smile, "Let's make a bet."

"OK," Robert replied. "What do you like in Harrisburg?"

"I love your home," Prince Albert said.

"I love your casino," said Robert, referring to the Monte Carlo Casino.

The two friends played as the crowd watching got larger and larger. It was a great game, and some of Robert's friends in the crowd signaled to Robert to let Prince Albert win, but it was not to be. Somehow, Robert won. *USA Today* reported that Robert had won the Monte Carlo Casino that day.

Before Prince Albert left Harrisburg, he'd written in the Morrison guest book, "How could I ever thank you enough. My three days with you were fabulous, you all were perfect hosts and what a party that was! ... The only negative point of the weekend was losing the Casino!! I have just one question: who should break the news to Dad?!! Thanks again. Much love. You're a great family."

The next few visits Robert made to Monaco, he joked, "How is my casino? Please take good care of it."

———————

LYNDA CARTER HAPPENED TO CALL ROBERT'S NEW YORK OFFICE when he was examining the singer, Connie Francis. The secretary called to Robert, "Dr. Morrison, you're wanted on the phone. Wonder Woman is making a movie and has to talk to you right away."

Lynda was filming the movie in three different locations and wanted to have a pair of contact lenses available for each place. Actually, she decided she really wanted three pairs for each location, something which Robert told her wasn't really necessary. Even just one extra pair would be plenty, but Lynda insisted.

When Robert hung up, Connie Francis said, "I'll have twelve pairs." Robert explained that twelve was more than anyone needed.

"Is Lynda Carter getting nine pairs?"

"Yes," Robert replied. "She wants three pairs at each of three locations."

"Then I'll have twelve. I want more than she has."


BEAUTIFUL MODEL CHERYL TIEG ONCE INTERVIEWED ROBERT ON the *Today Show.* When the interview was over, Tieg invited Robert to lunch. Dr. Morrison declined with regrets, having to rush to speak at the Mount Holly Women's Club lunch near Carlisle, Pennsylvania. A few hours later, Robert was speaking to the Women's Club, sharing the story, amidst much laughter and delight. It was the day the Women's Club had taken precedence over Cheryl Tieg.


ARLENE FRANCIS WAS A FAMOUS STAR OF THE STAGE AND SCREEN, as well as television and radio. She had a nationally syndicated radio program on WOR in New York City for many years, where she interviewed many of the great stars of the time. Once she said to Carol Channing, "I know you wear contact lenses and so do I.

I was wondering if you were hard to fit since you have those wonderful, big eyes?"

Ms. Channing replied, "I have the best eye doctor in the whole world and the challenge was his, and he has made me very happy. He's the very best."

"No," said Arlene Francis, "my eye doctor is the very best."

"But my eye doctor is Dr. Robert Morrison, and he is the best in the world."

Arlene Francis laughed, and she admitted that Carol Channing was right. You see, Ms. Francis's eye doctor was also Dr. Robert Morrison.

It was a pretty good free commercial for Dr. Morrison's practice, and many people phoned for appointments after that interview.

BARBARA WALTERS WAS DR. MORRISON'S PATIENT FOR OVER 22 years. The two became friends, and the Morrison's homes are adorned with her many wonderful gifts. Robert's daughter, Patty, wears a Cartier watch with an inscription on the back, "To RM from Barbara Walters."

Barbara went to Iran to interview the Shah. She sent a wonderful gift to Robert from Iran and mentioned that the Shah and she had talked about him since they were both Robert's patients.

ROBERT'S LIST OF ROYAL CLIENTS GREW TO INCLUDE THE GRAND Duchess Charlotte of Luxembourg, the Crown Prince of Saudi Arabia, and the Shah of Iran and his family, including Princess Sarvenaz, who even today visits the Morrisons at their home in Florida. Robert was becoming adept at traversing the political and social world abroad—but not without a few missteps.

One of these would occur after he started treating the Shah of Iran. Robert's innate love of learning tempted him to learn to speak

Iran's native language, Farsi. This, despite the fact that the Shah
and many in his family spoke English.

Later, he was in London to examine Mr. Adnan Kashoggi and
his wife. Mr. Kashoggi was then reported to be the richest man in
the world. At the time he'd contacted Robert, Mr. Kashoggi wasn't
allowed in the United States, and he asked Robert to come to London. When Robert agreed, Mr. Kashoggi sent him round trip tickets on the wonderful, now defunct Concorde. Robert recalls the
tickets were approximately $8,000.

Robert had read that Mr. Kashoggi's wife was from Iran, so
he decided to flash his Farsi. In the best accent he could muster, he
told her she was very beautiful.

She replied in Italian-accented English something that sounded like, "What zat you ah said?"

He replied in English, "I was trying to speak Farsi, since I
read that you were Iranian."

She blithely replied, "I do not speak Farsi. That was a different
wife."

It is permissible for a Muslim man to have as many as four
wives.


On another occasion Robert was asked to visit the marble
palace of the Shah of Iran's mother, the Queen Mother. This time
Robert was absolutely sure that she spoke Farsi but no English.
Robert would finally have the opportunity to practice his newly
acquired language skills. He'd met her and her grandson before,
so that seemed to be a safe topic.

In Farsi, Robert asked the Queen Mother about her grandson.

The Queen Mother laughed. Robert bit his tongue, trying to
figure out what in heaven's name he could have said that was so
funny. From across the large, ornate room an interpreter volun-

teered to help.

The interpreter joined them, and the Queen Mother and she exchanged some conversation in Farsi. Soon they were both laughing hysterically. When they were finally able to compose themselves, the interpreter told Robert he had said, "Your grandson is a jackass."

The Queen Mother then told the interpreter to please tell Robert something else for her. "Tell Dr. Morrison I agree with him."

Robert gave up the Farsi after that.

A TABLOID IN GERMANY REPORTED THAT THE PRINCE OF SAUDI Arabia had his eyes examined by Robert in Riyadh. The story described how the Rolls-Royce limo had picked Robert up at the airport in Saudi Arabia and took him to the Royal Palace, which was even described in the article in detail, with all its splendor. The story was picked up by the tabloids in South America.

The only problem with that story, Robert had never been to Saudi Arabia. The prince, however, did come to Harrisburg once, in a private jet with armed bodyguards. They all had dinner in the Morrisons' home.

After dinner, the prince asked if he could have a little tour of the Morrisons' home, as he liked it. Robert guided him around and eventually showed him the indoor pool, pointing out that both the room and the water were heated.

The prince felt the water and said, "It is not warm."

Robert replied, "Your fault. The price of oil is so high I can no longer afford to heat the water." They both laughed.

T HROUGH IT ALL, ROBERT'S OFFICE PRACTICE CONTINUED TO THRIVE. When he wasn't traveling, he taught Thursdays at the Pennsylvania College of Optometry as an associate professor of optometry and at New York Medical College as an assistant professor of ophthalmology. He was later appointed Professor of Ophthalmology at Albany Medical College and then Professor of Ophthalmology at Pennsylvania State University College of Medicine in Hershey, Pennsylvania.

At this point, the practice numbered 33 people, including an M.D., five doctors of optometry, opticians, secretaries, and technicians. The emphasis was to provide the best eye care for every patient whether it was a Hollywood star, a member of royalty, a high-ranking politician, or a charity case.

## 12

### KNIGHTHOOD

ROBERT WAS STILL AT HOME ONE FRIDAY MORNING WHEN THE phone rang. Based on the difference in time zones, it was six hours later in the Netherlands, so for Prince Bernhard, it was already afternoon.

They greeted each other and exchanged questions about each other's families. Then Prince Bernhard told Robert that Queen Juliana and he would like to knight him.

"Excuse me, I'm not sure I heard you right."

"Robert, we would like to make you a knight of the Order of St. John."

"I'm not sure I'd make a very good knight. They don't have them in the United States, P.B." (Prince Bernhard had a secretary who called him PB and suggested Robert do the same, so he did.) Harrisburg, Pennsylvania, wasn't exactly Camelot, and the movie theater was the closest Robert had ever gotten to knighthood. Certainly he had never run into anyone who was a Knight of the Round Table.

"It is an honor that Queen Juliana and I wish to convey to you."

"Then I accept gladly." Robert considered telling Ruth that she would have to soon call him "Your Majesty" and curtsy, but he decided not to press his luck.

That night, he and Ruth had the distinction of having the most unique conversation in Pennsylvania. While most couples were discussing what to have for dinner, Robert and Ruth discussed where they should choose to have the knighting ceremony.

Prince Bernhard had suggested they hold the formal ceremony at the palace in Amsterdam. As an alternative, he suggested the United Nations Building in New York City. There was a chapel there that could be used if that was Robert's choice.

Ruth and Robert pondered the situation. This would be an extraordinary event, a once-in-a-lifetime ceremony. If they chose the palace, the knighting would have all the pomp and circumstance that only the queen's royal situation could provide. Robert imagined the stately palace with its statuary, chandeliers, and velvet trappings. It would be an incredible setting for the ceremonial. On the other hand, it would be easier for friends and family to attend if the ceremony were to be held in New York. They eventually chose the All Faiths Chapel in the United Nations so that more of their friends and family could attend.

The local Harrisburg newspaper, *The Patriot-News*, interviewed Robert in order to do an article about his honor of being knighted by Queen Juliana. If the reporter thought he'd get an erudite answer about why Robert had been chosen to be Harrisburg's first and probably only knight, he didn't get the story.

"Why me?" was Robert's answer. "All I know is I was told to be there, wear my black tails, and bring my family and close friends."

The Tuesday of the ceremony, Ruth and Robert arrived with Jim and Patty, Robert's mother, and a small group of close friends. All Faiths Chapel at the United Nations was a relatively small religious area that was interdenominational so that all faiths could worship there, each in their own way.

Prince Bernhard was there to greet Robert and handed him

a red satin cape with a white collar and a white border on the sleeves. A bejeweled golden clasp held the cape on his neck.

The ceremony was everything Robert had seen in the movies. He knelt in front of Prince Bernhard who grasped a sword with a jeweled handle. A dignitary, complete with an old-fashioned monocle, read a passage from the New Testament.

In ages past, the recipient of the Knights of Malta confirmation required that the honoree be a member of Catholic royalty for four generations. Robert wasn't even Catholic.

It didn't bother the easygoing Robert, and his mother noted that all the words were beautiful and meaningful. She'd always been open-minded, and as young children, Robert and his siblings had all attended summer school at the nearby Lutheran Church. Their parents thought it was good to learn about every faith.

Fortunately, the qualifications had evolved and the requirements for knighthood had changed from those 900 years ago. Persons who weren't Catholic or even royal were eligible to be knighted. One had to be brave, a good warrior, charitable, or a poet—or merely someone who had done something outstanding in the world.

The answer to Robert's "why me?" question was clear to everyone, except himself. His credentials included countless contributions to eye care. They went beyond the introduction of the soft contact lens and his expertise that made him the eye doctor to royalty. He made it his life's work to bring healthy vision to everyone, and that included providing valuable services and charitable donations to the vision impaired throughout the world.

Prince Bernhard tapped the bejeweled sword on each of Robert's shoulders and conferred on him the honor of being one of the Knights of Malta, St. John of Jerusalem.

Flashbulbs popped and when the formal ceremony had finished, Robert joked in his usual self-deprecating manner, "Will I be called Sir Robert, or what?"

The dignitaries and guests adjourned to the sumptuous Hotel Pierre for a celebratory reception that included champagne, hors d' oeuvres, and special toasts to the new Sir Robert Morrison.

Robert later received a call from the White House in which the chief of protocol explained that since the time of the Revolution, when titled Englishmen still resided in the United States, it was acceptable for Americans to be knighted. It was also acceptable for them to use *Sir*, but in his effort to ensure that etiquette and decorum were observed, he made it clear that it was not considered acceptable to "hold yourself to be better than the next person."

The politician didn't know Robert's self-deprecating good humor, or he wouldn't have wasted his breath. The diplomatic passport Robert received as an adopted member of royalty was never used by Sir Robert Morrison. Neither did he adopt the *Sir* that knighthood conferred on him. He thought Sir was an English title, but he did enjoy the honor of having it. Robert had no plans to ever use it and would best not question it.

# 13

# A Jane Fonda
# Encounter Of The
# Worst Kind

R OBERT MORRISON HAD LOST ALL THE PATENT RIGHTS TO National Patent Development Company. At best, he could always say he was co-patent holder for all the soft contact lenses in the Western Hemisphere and a few other countries. In fact, much to Robert's chagrin, National Patent Development Company had even taken credit for bringing the soft lens patent to the United States at an industry presentation. They didn't mention Robert's crucial role in meeting Professor Wichterle, discussing the new material, exploring the potential for optical use with him, and experimenting with the HEMA polymer to perfect the soft contact lens.

Despite the fact that Robert had lost the patent rights on the original HEMA polymer, he was still experimenting with soft contact lenses. In order to offer his eye patients a better soft lens product, he had his own contact lens laboratory that made custom contact lenses. The product he created was based upon a unique lens design. The lenses themselves were made of a modified HEMA formula to which Robert had added N-vinyl pyrrolidone.

Robert's firm was named Morrison Laboratories, Inc., located in Harrisburg, Pennsylvania. It employed a staff of more than 100 people who worked three shifts around the clock making both rigid and soft contact lenses. The soft lenses were different than the original HEMA gel lenses because of the additive Robert had used.

Robert had also acquired a lab, Gordon Contact Lenses in Rochester, New York. The owner and operator, Dr. Stanley Gordon, made a soft contact lens called Aquaflex with Robert's input. It was also made from the original HEMA with the N-vinyl pyrrolidone added. The firm enjoyed excellent sales, and other lens companies purchased the lenses, added their profit margin, and resold them. All told, Robert began selling a lot of lenses. He personally received ten cents for each and every contact lens sold.

At the time, National Patent Development Company was issuing lawsuits against any and all contact lens companies that were manufacturing soft contact lenses, asserting it was an infringement on their patent. Other contact lens labs were being forced to pay royalties in order to manufacture and market the new soft lenses in the United States.

One day Robert received a letter in which National Patent Development threatened to sue his labs for patent infringement for manufacturing soft contact lenses. Other companies had agreed to pay royalties when threatened—but Robert saw red.

He grabbed the telephone and dialed Martin Pollock's number. Robert may have been ousted as a patent holder, but he was convinced he was in the right to be able to make his own version of soft contact lenses. Morally, there was no way he would give up the ability to create soft lenses himself.

Pollock admitted that the National Patent Development Company could never have brought the patent to the United States without Robert. Pollock said to Robert on the phone, "You are correct. We should acknowledge this and will do so in future presentations." And Pollock and his company actually did.

As far as the lawsuit against Robert was concerned, Robert knew what he would say, and in no uncertain terms, he laid out the ground rules to Pollock. "I don't think you want to sue me or my company. I know too much."

Pollock dropped the case.

Robert eventually sold Morrison Laboratories, inc., to Union Corporation, which was listed on the New York Stock Exchange. When Union Corp. bought Morrison Laboratories, they asked Robert to acquire other rigid contact lens labs. Subsequently, he purchased several contact lens laboratories which were gathered under the umbrella company called Union Optics, which became part of Union Corporation. Robert became Chairman of the Board of Union Optics and Vice President of Union Corporation.

After the sale, Robert maintained an eye practice in the building he owned, and he rented the lower level basement area to Union Corporation for use as a laboratory. One day a New York labor union appeared on the site with the goal of convincing the Union Corporation employees that they should organize and get better benefits. The employees voted to strike, and several people picketed Robert's office building off and on for three years. Amazingly, during those three years, Robert's eye practice never suffered. His patients, including the governor and lieutenant governor of Pennsylvania, simply passed the picket line and continued to see him.

One day Jane Fonda and her then-husband came to the picketing and approximately 100 people protested on television. Robert arrived at work and decided that he would simply stay inside the building and avoid any confrontation. It was not his style to become involved in things that were none of his business.

As he watched the events unfolding outside, however, Jane Fonda mentioned him by name. Basically, she told the audience that Dr. Robert Morrison was the eye doctor to the Shah of Iran, one of the richest men in the world.

"Does he share any of the wealth with you!?" Fonda cried out to the crowd.

The organizers took the hint and began shouting. "No! No!"

Robert was dismayed by the attack that was not only completely unjustified, but based on misinformation. He sprinted outside, and while trying to be polite, he told Jane Fonda as diplomatically as he could, "Miss Fonda, you are a fine actress. Many people admire your acting ability. I could not settle this strike even if it took just one cent to satisfy. I do not own the company. It is owned by the Union Corporation. I practice here and that is all. How in the world am I to share the Shah's wealth with these workers?"

Robert remembers her ignoring his statement in order to continue her harangue.

"He refused to share the wealth and expects you to end the strike and go to work! Will you!?"

The union organizers shouted, "No! No!"

The news cameras were there, capturing the event for the television news. The people on the picket line were at first involved with Union Corporation, but later the union organizers just picked up people at the unemployment offices. The day of Jane Fonda's appearance, the union had picked up about 100 shouting people for the benefit of the television cameras.

When the union organizers shouted "No!", they led the mob like cheerleaders, repeating the chant so it would appear as though many angry, shouting people were there. Just minutes after Jane Fonda left the site, the entire mob dispersed and the four or five picketers, none of whom worked in the lab, put down their signs and strolled around the building.

Many of the people who used to work for Robert and later moved on to Union Corporation, found other jobs, but often they made it known that when the strike was settled, they would like to come back to work there. As it turned out, Jane Fonda's influence caused the Union Corporation to rethink its location in Harrisburg. They moved the lab to Rochester, New York, where the employees were hired. In the opinion of some of the former lab workers, it was Jane Fonda who had been responsible for their losing their jobs as she championed a cause against Robert Morrison, inflamed controversy in the community, and caused Union Corporation to move the lab from Harrisburg to Rochester.

Still later, the courts became involved. Robert was forced to hire a law firm, and during the legal process, he repeated to the judge the fact that he didn't own the company. He'd sold it a few years ago and therefore could not settle the strike. Robert's lawyer contended that the remarks on television were detrimental to Robert Morrison personally.

The judge asked the union's New York lawyers to question Robert's lawyer. In addition, he insisted that they provide an explanation of why the union was continuing to picket Robert's offices.

The union's lawyers simply said, "No questions."

The judge ruled that the picketing must stop immediately, but Jane Fonda had already lost Robert as a fan.

# 14

## THE WORLD'S HEARTIEST BREAKFAST

W HEN ROBERT MADE HIS REGULAR VISITS TO SOESTDIJK PALACE to see Queen Juliana and Prince Bernhard, he normally stayed at the Amstel Hotel as a guest of the royal family. Flowers and gourmet treats would welcome him to the room, which he considered just another sign of kindness and the considerate nature the royal couple showed him.

As the professional relationship changed to friendship, Robert was eventually invited to stay at Soestdijk Palace itself. Being invited to the palace was an honor that was reserved for special guests.

Ruth was with Robert the first time they were invited to stay there. They were shown to a suite that was beautifully decorated right down to the personalized accessories. To ensure that guests could perhaps brag a little and assure their friends and family that they had, indeed, stayed in the Royal Palace, the desk was stocked with stationery and matches that bore beautiful photographs of the palace.

On that first visit, as Robert and Ruth were settling in and admiring their surroundings, they happened to notice a menu card sitting on the desk. The printed menu policy asked them to please review the breakfast offerings, make their selection, and leave the list on the door for the maid to retrieve.

The list covered an entire page. There were eggs from hard boiled to scrambled, soft boiled to fried. The breakfast meats included bacon, sausage, ham, and steak. Fruits included everything from strawberries to kiwis to bananas and more. An assortment of cheeses were offered as were a long list of cereals, several types of muffins, whole wheat toast, white toast, and croissants. There were at least eight types of juice including orange, tomato, papaya, and grapefruit. There was coffee in regular or decaffeinated and a selection of teas. It was an impressively long list fit for a queen—or the guests of one.

Ruth and Robert studied the list. It all sounded delicious, and they had some tough choices to make. One other thought occurred to each of them. It was their first visit to the Royal Palace, and they wanted to be polite.

"We don't want to appear greedy. Let's keep it simple and just order scrambled eggs and toast. No meat or cheese," Ruth suggested.

"We could have orange juice and coffee," Robert said.

"That would be fine."

They agreed eggs and toast plus the beverages would suffice.

The next morning a knock on the door announced that their breakfast had arrived. Robert threw on his robe and opened the door. Four butlers waited in the hall, each with a professional food cart on wheels.

Each cart was piled high with covered platters of all sizes and shapes. The server proceeded to set the table in their suite with a tablecloth, fine China, and silver place settings. The trolleys rolled in, covered with every type of breakfast dish.

"But we only ordered scrambled eggs and toast," Robert mumbled.

Every type of egg and breakfast bread and other food was there—except for scrambled eggs and toast, orange juice, and coffee.

Robert looked at the sheet of paper tucked into one corner of a tray. He read it more carefully.

"Please mark the breakfast items you do NOT want on this sheet."

They ate well that morning, but Robert was thoroughly embarrassed and had no idea how to broach the topic with Prince Bernhard when they met later. Did he dare say that he and Ruth were not the gluttons that their mistaken breakfast order would imply?

Eventually, Robert got the royal system down pat, and his stays at the palace made him a royal fixture of sorts when he visited Queen Juliana and Prince Bernhard each year. The visits included the eye exams, but their growing friendship occupied the majority of the time.

One morning during one of the visits, Prince Bernhard came to Robert's room at the palace immediately after breakfast. The two men began with the usual host and guest pleasantries, the prince asking if Robert enjoyed the breakfast. Of course, every time this ritual played out, Robert cringed. He would never be allowed to forget the time he and Ruth had ordered enough to feed a small country.

"It was delicious, as usual."

The prince sat in one of the overstuffed chairs, and Robert offered him coffee from the breakfast decanter. They discussed mail and somehow the conversation switched to letter openers. The prince took one of the knives that was apparently the official silverware from the tray and gave it to Robert for use on his desk as a letter opener. It still sits on his desk beside his home computer.

Extravagant gifts were to become the norm. The Rolls-Royce from Queen Juliana was, of course, one of the most elaborate gifts anyone could receive. However, the generous royals gave Robert and Ruth an array of other gifts over the years including works of art, a silver tray, gold coins, and many rugs. Robert received a pair of cuff links set with star sapphires.

One of the most meaningful gifts was a bracelet watch which the royal couple offered Robert as a gift to Ruth. The piece was part of the crown jewels, and Queen Juliana included a handwritten note explaining the historical importance of this particular piece of jewelry.

"This was given to my mother, Queen Wilhelmina, at her coronation by her mother, Queen Emma. My mother then gave it to me, Juliana, at my coronation, and I now give it to Ruth Morrison."

The ornate bracelet opened to reveal a small watch with Roman numerals. The reverse side of the watch was a regal purple shade, imbedded with small pearls. The watch was wound with a small key. Robert tucked the watch carefully into the side pocket of his briefcase. He would guard this carefully.

At dinner that evening, the topic turned to the unique bracelet watch and the key. "I wouldn't want to lose that small item," Robert told them. "I've put it into an envelope to keep it safe."

"It took a year to have the key made," the queen commented.

"Yes," added Bernhard, leaning toward Robert. "So if the damn thing does not work, send it back to us."

"What was that, Bernhard?" asked the queen. Robert had noticed that she had a slight hearing loss, and she'd missed her husband's swear term. Robert wondered if Bernhard would clean up the language for his wife, the queen.

Prince Bernhard merely repeated his statement, more loudly this time. "I said, if the damn thing doesn't work, send it back to us."

Queen Juliana looked at Robert. Not to be beaten at hospitality or emphasis, she added, "If the *goddamn* thing does not work, please send it back to us."

At home, Robert presented the bracelet watch to Ruth who was awed by the gift. For the most part, they planned to keep it in a safety deposit box in their bank. Knowing Ruth would want to wear it occasionally and show it to friends and family, however, they needed to get the watch appraised for insurance purposes.

Robert asked the Metropolitan Museum of Art in New York to appraise the bracelet. At first the appraisers were stymied. Since the watch included some of the crown jewels, it was extremely unique. Nothing comparable existed. Eventually they appraised the bracelet watch at $250,000.

The museum, aware of the bracelet's unique history, asked if Ruth would donate it to that institution upon her death. Ruth couldn't agree. She wanted to leave the precious memento to their daughter, Patty. It was a personal gift and a memento that Ruth wanted to remain in the family.

Unfortunately, something happened to this precious gift. Friends had often asked to see the special jewelry—the bracelet watch, the Shah's gold portrait, and other items—so the Morrisons had a security firm, a very reliable one, build a safe into a wall at their home. The safe was well hidden, or so they thought.

One weekend when they were visiting New York City, their home was broken into. The thieves managed to override the house's burglar alarm and found the so-called hidden safe. The police offered the theory that the thieves may have simply used a Geiger counter to locate it. The entire safe—a heavy one at that—was stolen and never recovered. The bracelet watch, along with engraved coins from the Shah of Iran, disappeared.

The only thing left of the precious bracelet watch was the letter in Queen Juliana's own handwriting offering it to Ruth. The letter had not been in the safe.

WHEN THE MORRISONS VISITED THE PALACE, ROBERT AND Prince Bernhard often spent time playing golf. Ruth and the prince's bodyguard walked along with Robert and the prince on the golf course. Afterwards, at the Clubhouse, the prince would open a bottle of special wine he'd sent over to ensure he'd have only the finest for his guests and himself.

One time Prince Bernhard phoned Robert in Harrisburg and asked him if he'd ever seen the Grand Prix of Monaco. When Robert said that he hadn't, the prince suggested, as normally as most people meet for lunch down the street, that Robert fly to London and meet him at the elegant Claridge's Hotel before going on to Nice and then Monaco.

Robert did. They met in London the next morning, and the prince flew them in a private plane from London to Nice. A general in the Dutch Air Force was with them, and Robert supposed he could have been there to fly the plane if needed, but it wasn't at all necessary. After all, the prince had been a pilot in World War II for the Royal Air Force.

At one point during the flight, Prince Bernhard told one of his aides to bring Robert into the cockpit. Robert grabbed his camera. When he arrived, the prince was viewing the centerfold of *Playboy* magazine. In jest, Robert snapped a picture.

The prince smiled and asked, "Do you think you got it?"

"No, you might have moved."

"Try another."

He posed and Robert snapped the shutter. That shot came out perfectly, and it became one of the highlights of Robert's photo albums.

The two stayed the night in Nice, and the next day, drove the 30 minutes it took to get to Monaco in the prince's snappy Jaguar convertible. A driver had brought the car from Holland to the Nice Airport specifically so the prince would have that sporty vehicle to drive over the curving mountain roads to Monaco. Prince Bernhard told Robert he needed to sit in the passenger seat, and his aide squeezed into what Robert considered a much too small back seat. Despite the hot day, Prince Bernhard donned sporty driving gloves, and they took off driving like the Grand Prix drivers that they intended to view.

As they rounded some of the bends on the incredibly curving roads that wound high above the Atlantic surf, Robert had the fleeting thought that he would die on that road. But at least, he thought, he'd be leaving the world while he was on an adventure with "a nice fellow in a nice part of the world."

His tension was evident to the aide who, at one point, held his fingers to his lips to indicate that Robert shouldn't speak. Later, he told him that any inference—quivering in fear obviously counted—that the prince was a poor driver, was unacceptable. Europeans were proud of their driving skills and fast driving was greatly admired.

At the Grand Prix, they were invited to join Prince Rainier and Princess Grace in the Royal Box. The couple had graciously provided a special bottle of wine, which Robert knew was one of the best he'd ever sipped. The noise was tremendous as the cars careened around the city streets, closed especially for the race. The crowd surrounding them was busily photographing the cars and using tape recorders to capture the unique roar the vehicles created in the enclosed spaces.

Robert was thoroughly engrossed in the atmosphere when Prince Bernhard nudged him. He pointed to the distinguished Prince Rainier and the elegant Princess Grace. Despite the thundering noise of the race cars, they had fallen asleep.

# 15

## THE SHAH OF IRAN

ROBERT AND RUTH WERE PREPARING FOR THEIR SUMMER vacation with their children, Jim and Patty. It was to be a special family trip to France where they would visit the northern coast near the resort town of Deauville, known particularly for its horse racing. They were to explore the historic Normandy area where the Americans landed during World War II, visit the American Cemetery, and spend time together enjoying the special ambiance of the countryside. They were all looking forward to the trip.

The phone rang just four days before they were to leave. On the other end of the line was one of the Shah of Iran's aides. Robert took the call, and Ruth could hear the surprise in his voice. His half of the conversation told her that something important was being discussed, something that probably affected her and the children. Knowing Robert's impulsive behavior when it came to jetting off at the request of royal clients, she grew wary but was relieved to hear that he was apparently defending the family's vacation time.

"I'm sorry, but my family and I are planning to leave on vacation in a few days."

There was a pause.

"I suppose we could visit afterwards." Robert was tentative.

That made Ruth nervous. "We will call right back."

"The Shah," Robert said to Ruth. "He wants me to examine his eyes."

"We've already made plans ... the children have school off, Bobby. We can't just change the family vacation." Ruth was disappointed, and though normally patient, the last minute change was not something she would gladly agree to, especially when it concerned the children.

"I know. I know."

The phone rang again while they were still discussing whether they could manage to visit the Shah after their trip to France.

"Dr. Morrison, the Shah would like to invite your family to vacation here in Iran instead of France. You would be special guests of the Shah."

Robert looked at Ruth.

"We may have an offer too good to refuse."

THE OFFER WAS, INDEED, TOO GOOD TO PASS UP. THEY COULD VISIT France some other time, but the opportunity to be the personal guests of one of the richest men in the world was one that didn't come along too often.

The four Morrisons boarded a jet for Iran, flying first class as the Shah's guests. They were met by a limousine in Iran. Robert easily handled the eye exams that the Shah had requested. As usual, he never billed any members of the royal family for his services. The boy from Harrisburg felt honored to be at any royal palace, and he billed none of them.

After that, the Morrisons were offered a luxurious tour of the country. The Shah even provided a personal helicopter with a pilot and tour guide.

They stayed in the finest hotels and were treated to gourmet meals. The trip was everything they could have dreamed of and more.

Among the many places they visited was Pahlavi University, named for the Shah whose given name was Reza Pahlavi. Professors from all over the world taught there, including Americans from Johns Hopkins in Baltimore and the University of Pennsylvania in Philadelphia.

As though he weren't doing enough, at one point the Shah asked if he could possibly do Robert a favor.

"Actually, Your Majesty, I am just honored to be here."

But then Robert recalled his two nephews. Each was a premed student who had dreams of medical school. The Shah called over Mr. Alam, who was one of his best friends and headed the Pahlavi School of Medicine. The medical school in Shiraz used American professors, teaching in English. It allowed five American students to enroll each year. The Shah spoke to Mr. Alam who then told Robert that if he sent his two nephews to Shiraz, they would be admitted to the med school.

One nephew wanted to be a psychologist, not a physician, and did not enroll in the school despite Robert's insistence that the opportunity was rare and should be strongly considered. The other, however, did spend two years in Shiraz, then returned to graduate from medical school in the states and became a retinal surgeon.

Robert would continue to make visits to Iran, and his workload increased since it included the Shah's large extended family. The visits to the palace of the Shah's elder sister, Princess Shams, and her husband, the then minister of culture and art, Mehrdad Pahlbod, would be particularly memorable.

The Morvarid Palace was built in 1966, several years after Frank Lloyd Wright's death, by a son-in-law and first apprentice to Frank Lloyd Wright named Wesley Peters. Many engineers and architects believe the palace may have actually been designed by the famous American architect himself during his lifetime.

It was built on a large site near an artificial lake and consisted of two intersecting domes with a series of other buildings creating an enclosed area of over 50,000 square feet. One distinct feature of the structure was a spiral ramp that rose high into the air, all the way to the Princess's bedroom, where it culminated in a spiral ziggurat.

The princess was reportedly so happy when she saw the original plans for the palace, she burst into tears and said it was everything she dreamed of since she was a little girl. The paintings and designs in the palace were circular; the colors of the floor, walls, and furniture were dazzling, and every square inch of the huge space seemed to be decorated. Plexiglass was used frequently throughout the palace, along with glass and crystal.

Robert recalls numerous levels of the palace were accessed in an unusual variety of ways. There were sloped corridors, ramps, and staircases. Robert never observed the concept of four walls throughout the entire palace. It was definitely unique and fit for a princess.

Robert remembers his first visit to the palace. He wanted to take the princess's intraocular pressure to look for glaucoma. At the time, the best way to do it was to have the patient lie down. The princess went to her bedroom to lie down on her bed, and Robert used a Schiotz to examine her. When he did, 15 small dogs who seemed to resent Robert being there, snapped at him numerous times.

On another visit, Robert was in the midst of his examination when a servant told the princess a representative from Cartier in France had arrived. Princess Shams started to look at some fabulous pieces of jewelry while Robert kept doing his work.

Robert stopped and said that he was certainly in no hurry and would gladly wait until Her Highness's visit with the man from Paris was completed. The princess told Robert to continue his work and she continued looking at the jewels.

Robert said, "Your Highness, I came halfway around the world to do my work, and I want very much to do it well. I am in no hurry and will gladly wait."

An aide called Robert aside and said, "It is Her Highness's wish that you continue your work while she is viewing the jewels. That is her decision to make, not yours."

On yet another visit, the princess said to Robert, "You have done so much for me. I would like to give you a present."

Robert said, "No thanks. It is a great honor just to be here."

Later, an aid told Robert that the princess really wanted to do something for him. Robert said, "I would love to take some pictures of this lovely palace."

The aid spoke to someone, and they said that it was not possible to take pictures because of security reasons. Later, however, the princess said she hated to say no to Robert and it was OK—but to be sure the pictures didn't get into the wrong hands. Robert was told that his pictures were, at that time, the only ones taken of the palace.

Once, Robert was able to take his nephew, Andrew Eller, along with him to Morvarid Palace. At one point, Robert and Andrew wandered upstairs, ascending a beautiful, elegant, plexiglass stairway. They eventually entered an area with two velvet chairs, each with a royal seal on back. One was for the Shah of Iran, and the other was for Her Majesty Queen Farah.

Robert had been told in the past not to sit on the Shah's chair. Where His Majesty puts his royal derriere, no one else could put theirs.

Robert said to Andy, "I will sit in the Shah's chair. You snap the picture."

Andy said, "Please, Uncle Bob. Don't!" But Robert did it anyway, and Andy quickly snapped the picture, which he still has.

THE SHAH WAS GENEROUS WITH GIFTS WHICH INCLUDED A LARGE

piece of gold, four inches in diameter, that was engraved with the Shah's picture. One time Robert admired a painting by Mr. Tabrizi, a painter who is greatly admired and well-known in Iran. After Robert returned home, the Shah sent the painting to him.

Eventually, he was to receive four other Tabrizi paintings plus three Persian rugs. Two of the Persian rugs were Nain, and the all silk one was Qum.

When Robert questioned an Iranian authority on carpets, he was told "Americans show wealth with a Cadillac. In Iran it's shown with a Nain." The man referred to a type of Persian carpet, considered among the best in the world. The soft wool, Nain, is extravagantly designed and crafted with a curvilinear pattern bordered in silk.

Robert continued to make regular visits to the Shah's palace. From time to time, Robert brought some members of his staff from Harrisburg to assist him, but he always examined the Shah's eyes himself.

The two men had a special relationship, one that was unusual to find in the royal household, in that Robert would blithely speak his mind as he would with any friend. This, despite the fact that the Shah's staff made it clear that everyone dealing with the Shah should agree with him on every point. It was the ultimate yes man situation, but one which Robert couldn't quite manage.

When they discussed issues—political, artistic, or social— Robert would find himself blurting out a casual comment such as, "Come on, Your Majesty, you can't be serious. You don't really believe that! If you do, I sincerely disagree with you and I would like to tell you why ..."

One time an aide quickly stepped behind the Shah and put his fingers to his lips, gesturing wildly to Robert that he should not disagree with His Majesty. He waved his hands, palms facing Robert, indicating that he should cease, but Robert continued and was convinced that the Shah enjoyed their conversations. Perhaps he considered it a refreshing change and gave Robert, as a foreigner, some leeway that his staff or family might not otherwise have had.

In any case, Robert was sure the Shah looked forward to his visits, their discussions, and the fact that he would share his point of view even if it was much different than his. He also found out the Shah was not impressed by the lack of American interest and knowledge of his native land and culture.

"We Iranians know very much about the United States and its cultures, but I never met an American who knew anything about our Persian culture ... perhaps only that excellent caviar comes from the Caspian Sea."

The Shah referred to his favorite caviar from the albino sturgeon. It consisted of golden eggs that were served with ice cold vodka.

Robert couldn't resist replying to the Shah's remark by saying, "Your Majesty, how would you feel if I quoted *The Rubaiyat of Omar Khayyam*?"

The Shah smiled. "I would be favorably impressed."

Robert quoted the verse as he remembered it. "Here with a loaf of bread underneath the bough, a flask of wine, a book of verse—and thou, beside me singing in the wilderness—oh, wilderness is paradise enough."

The Shah enjoyed this banter so much that when Robert returned to his room in the palace, he discovered a beautiful silk Persian carpet made in Qum, a city famous for silk rugs. The rug was bordered with quotes from Omar Khayyam. When Robert thanked the Shah, they spoke further of Omar Khayyam, probably the most famous of Persian poets who lived about 1000 AD.

Khayyam had been translated by many people, but Robert's favorite translation was by the Englishman Edward Fitzgerald. Robert told the Shah that Omar Khayyam was obsessed with women, wine, poetry, and nature. According to Robert, he rarely wrote a verse that didn't include a woman and wine.

The friendship grew and extended to some other members of the Shah's family. The Shah's brother had a daughter, Princess Sarvenaz, who became so close to Robert and Ruth that she began calling them Uncle Bob and Auntie Ruthie. Her name meant tall, slender tree or beautiful woman. She lived up to it, as Sarvenaz was not only beautiful but extremely intelligent. She attended Harvard in the United States, earning a masters degree. She still visits the Morrisons at their home in Florida.

## 16

### RADIO, TELEVISION, AND A BOOK

ROBERT HAD HIS SHARE OF FAME OVER THE YEARS, WITH countless appearances on television and radio shows. One television show in particular stands out because it was not merely an interview or talk show but a game show. Robert was asked to appear on the television show, which was popular in the 60's, called *What's My Line?*.

The objective of the show was to introduce a famous person who wasn't readily recognized but who was accomplished in a special field, whether technical or creative, professional or service-oriented. The interesting twist was that the show would include two other people, impostors, who also claimed to be the famous person.

Each person, real or impostor, would be presented with questions from celebrity panelists about themselves and their specialty. The expert would answer truthfully. The impostors could fake facts or out-and-out lie in order to assert their expertise. The celebrities would eventually have to guess which of the three people was the real expert.

*What's My Line?* paid Robert's way to New York City where he stayed as their guest at the elegant St. Moritz Hotel on Central Park, since torn down. At the television studio, they installed him in a room where he met the Dr. Robert Morrison impostors who were to pretend to be experts on vision care, one of the co-developers of the soft contact lens, and the man who treated the world's royalty and celebrities as patients and often as friends.

Robert had just an hour to teach his *clones* whatever he thought they might have to know in order to skillfully lie. Naturally, they had to appear knowledgeable about vision, a field that Robert had studied for years.

Robert found out quickly that his impostors had little or no biology knowledge. He gave them a crash course in vision, including two facts that later proved helpful. First, he told the impostors that the correct name for nearsightedness was *myopia*. Second, he mentioned that the name for a medical or eye condition in which the cause could not be ascertained was known as a condition of "unknown etiology."

During the show, one of the panelists actually asked an impostor, "What causes nearsightedness?"

Robert nearly gave himself away with laughter when the impostor very adroitly replied, "Myopia is of unknown etiology."

As for the real Dr. Robert Morrison, he couldn't tell even the slightest lie and had to sign an affidavit to that effect; however, he was allowed to hesitate, pause as though puzzled, or try any theatrics he could muster in order to fool the celebrity panelists.

Robert enjoyed the challenge. One regular celebrity on the show was Peggy Cass, who recused herself from the panel because she was actually one of Robert's patients. She'd even visited the Morrisons and stayed at their home.

Of the other celebrity panelists, only Kitty Carlisle guessed Robert correctly as the person who introduced the soft contact lens and was the vision expert on call for royals and celebrities around the world.

NEWS AND TALK SHOWS WERE AMONG THE DOZENS ON WHICH

Robert appeared. Diane Sawyer interviewed Dr. Morrison for the *CBS Morning News* and it resulted in a rather straight forward interview regarding his career. He also appeared on the *The Mike Douglas Show,* talking about his fascinating experiences with royalty. During the commercial break, Mike Douglas happened to ask Robert if he had ever been honored to be an overnight guest in any of the palaces where he worked.

Robert, of course, said, "Yes, many of them." He named two, including the Royal Palace in Belgium and the Royal Palace in the Netherlands. He told Mike Douglas he had never been an overnight guest of the Grimaldis in Monaco. Instead, he was always offered a prestigious hotel suite with a balcony overlooking the famous Monaco Harbor. The harbor was filled with some of the largest yachts anywhere, belonging to royalty and multimillionaires from around the world.

Although Dr. Morrison would not confirm this part of the story, Mike Douglas supposedly asked Robert why he had never slept in the palace in Monaco and Robert quipped, "If Princess Grace knew I was down the hall in my PJ's, she might not trust herself."

Douglas roared with laughter.

"Dr. Morrison, we'll be back on the air in ten seconds. I'll ask you that question again, and I want you to answer exactly the same way."

"No way! I can't do that. It would be my last visit to Monaco!"

Mike Douglas was disappointed, but Robert's decorum and that of Princess Grace remained intact.

FOR YEARS, ROBERT HAD CONSIDERED WRITING A BOOK THAT WOULD share his expertise with the average person who wore contact lenses or was considering wearing them. At that time, in the mid 70's, contact lenses were still relatively new on the market. Robert had fielded hundreds of questions from patients who wanted to know everything about contact lenses, from whether or not contacts would be good for their vision problem, to how to insert and remove them, to how long they could wear them safely, to how to care for contacts properly.

One morning he woke up early, as was his habit. It was only a little after 4:00 a.m., but he simply decided it was time he wrote the book, and he would write it that day.

Robert had written scientific papers before but never anything as involved or lengthy as a book. This one was to be for the public, not an eye professional or scientist. He decided that a simple question and answer format would work best and be the clearest way to explain the subject to the layman.

He began writing by considering all the questions he'd been asked. He added to that all the questions that would provide the answers he knew the contact lens wearers should have so they could properly take care of their eyes and their lenses.

He sat at his desk and was soon so engrossed that he didn't want to stop working. He became like a man possessed, so determined to get all the facts down in writing that he kept going until midnight. By then, his question and answer manuscript was completed.

The book was published by HRL Publishing Corporation in hardcover as *The Contact Lens Book* in 1976. The dust jacket noted Robert J. Morrison's credentials, including his prominent private practice, his professorships, his role in the invention of the soft contact lens, his knighting, and his frequent guest appearances on television and radio.

The book sold well as a hardcover edition, then Simon and Schuster bought the paperback rights to it. Six months later they published a paperback version that sold tens of thousands of copies. The American Library Association selected it as a recommended purchase for librarians. Dr. Robert Morrison could now add *author* to his long list of credentials.

## 17

---

## GROWING PRACTICE,
## CONSULTING, AND TEACHING

I n 1983 ROBERT SOLD MORRISON LABORATORIES, A SOFT and rigid contact lens company, in order to lecture and direct research in other areas of vision. He also acted as a consultant to the international cosmetic firm Revlon.

Revlon was making forays into the field of contact lenses and their care. It had purchased a contact lens company from an optometrist in San Diego who had created a good selling lens called Hydrocurve. Revlon also purchased a firm called Barnes Hind, the largest company to provide contact lens solutions. It made a good fit for Revlon.

Revlon trusted Robert's input, but they often requested his assistance too late. At one point, Revlon was excited about the possibility of developing a bifocal contact lens, so it purchased the rights to one from a man in New York. The bifocal lens, however, did not function well at all. Finally, Revlon asked Robert to determine the problem. When he studied the lens, Robert advised Revlon that it would never work, and he suggested the company needed to stop marketing it.

He also requested that the company ask his opinion a little sooner since it appeared that in every case his consulting skills were being used, it was already too late to save the firm from a mistake. Robert had another reason for requesting that Revlon use him sooner and more often. His contract paid him well for his consulting services; Robert actually considered it too well. Most people would never complain they were making too much money for not enough work, but Robert's sense of fairness insisted that he provide more service to Revlon to earn that fee. He often told Revlon, "I am overpaid and underused." Revlon, however, saw the need to have the noted specialist on call and were perfectly willing to pay for the privilege.

Later, Revlon received FDA approval to market an extended wear Hydrocurve lens that had tremendous marketing potential. Its importance was underscored by the fact that the wearer would be able to sleep with the lens on for as long as 30 days.

The freedom from daily care was a giant step forward in convenience. Busy contact lens wearers could avoid having to follow the nightly routine of removal and cleaning of the lens, and they would wake up with clear vision and ready to start their day. It was a boon to travelers, people with erratic schedules, and anyone who simply didn't want the daily hassle involved in most contact lens care.

Revlon called a meeting on the new extended wear Hydrocurve lens in New York and asked Dr. Morrison to chair the meeting. Robert had approved of the extended wear lens, verified it was good, but he urged practitioners to be aware that FDA approval did not mean every patient should be permitted to wear the new lens overnight. Robert cited a professor at the University of California in Berkeley, Robert Mandell, O.D., Ph.D., who had presented a study that showed the cornea swells slightly when a person is sleeping, and when the cornea is deprived of oxygen, it swells even more. The swelling, called edema, was a possible danger to the cornea, so Robert urged practitioners who prescribed extended wear lenses to watch for potential problems in their patients.

Revlon representatives approved of the warning and even

praised Robert for trying to make O.D.s and M.D.s aware of potential problems. The care and attention of the professionals prescribing the new extended wear lens would be to Revlon's benefit since any problems experienced by the contact lens wearers would reflect poorly and might result in loss of FDA approval.

As it turned out, the FDA approval was eventually rescinded anyway. The search for an extended wear lens continued, and other firms gained approval for 30-day lenses by adding silicone to the lens material, which allowed oxygen to pass through easily. The oxygen was the secret since the cornea needed it to maintain its healthy function.

The need for extended wear lenses became more important in later years when the FDA approved laser surgery procedures. Robert considered the extended wear lens a safer, non-surgical means of correcting the refractive errors of the eye without the risk of surgery. His opinion had always been that if the contact lens is not comfortable due to a poor fitting, allergies, or any other cause, the patient should just take them off. But if any form of surgery resulted in poor night vision, dry eyes, or other problems, then it was too late. The surgery had been done and that was that.

Bausch & Lomb also promoted an extended wear lens, and the company was sued by CIBA Vision and lost, forcing B & L to cease selling those lenses for the time being. Bausch & Lomb and Johnson & Johnson are presently marketing extended wear contact lenses with FDA approval.

THE MORRISON ASSOCIATES PRACTICE IN HARRISBURG HAD SERVED tens of thousands of patients, making it one of the largest contact lens specialty practices in the country. Robert sold his eye care practice to Polyclinic Hospital, one of the two major hospitals in Harrisburg at the time. The hospitals later merged and became known as Pinnacle Health Care. However, knowing the power and credibility of the name, the hospital continued to manage the eye care practice under the name *The Morrison Associates.*

It was the first time in Pennsylvania that a private optometric practice was purchased and run by a hospital, and the deal made Dr. Robert Morrison several million dollars richer. This wasn't bad for a man who had never considered financial gain as his prime motivation.

Polyclinic Hospital requested a ten year contract which required Robert to be present in the clinic's offices for a minimum of 36 days a year. Robert went that extra yard as usual, however, and would show up in the eye care office more often than that. After almost four decades of devoting himself to caring for eyes and developing new products that would improve vision, Dr. Robert Morrison was not about to completely retire from the field he knew and loved.

Robert retained his private practice in New York and continued to teach at the Pennsylvania College of Optometry, Albany Medical College, and New York Medical College.

Eventually, he sold the New York City practice to Dr. Tonia Mortelliti, who named it The Morrison and Mortelliti Associates. Robert still lectures at the Pennsylvania State University College of Medicine in Hershey, Pennsylvania, and occasionally visits the New York office to see a special, long-term patient, or perhaps royalty or celebrities.

Robert's entrepreneurial and creative nature were soon to kick into high gear again, leading him to develop another innovative product. This time, he would be proud to join in a business venture with his now adult son, Jim Morrison, who was busy shaping his own version of a career in eye care.

# 18

# EYEGLASSES FOR THE DISADVANTAGED

ACCORDING TO THE WORLD HEALTH ORGANIZATION, IN 1993, one billion people around the world needed eyeglasses to improve their vision but didn't have access to them, largely due to cost. To Robert, with his extraordinary concern for eye care, this situation was a terrible waste of the ability for those people to enjoy a full life. Their lack of good vision often resulted in difficulties in participating actively in life or enjoying the simplest of pleasures. Even more important, that lack of good vision often hindered their ability to be educated or earn a decent living. Without good vision, those people couldn't see blackboards, read for education or pleasure, perform fine craft work, or drive safely.

The problem of how to provide affordable vision improvement to the less fortunate had been simmering in Robert's head for years. What percolated to the surface was a totally new idea that he thought would revolutionize eye care. Ironically, the idea was a reversal from the advancements he'd made in soft contact lenses. His newest invention reverted back to eyeglasses.

They weren't just any eyeglasses, however. The special design would allow even the disadvantaged, in any part of the world, to see clearly. More importantly, the cost would make it possible for virtually anyone to afford them because each pair of eyeglasses could be provided for under a dollar.

The advantage of eyeglasses in third world environments is the fact that sanitary conditions don't matter as much as they do with contact lens care. Unlike contact lenses, the lenses of eyeglasses don't touch the cornea.

The idea came together one day as Robert was fitting a pair of round eyeglasses' frames, positioning the lenses in order to exactly match the prescription that would improve the patient's vision. He knew, of course, that the lenses had to be in the right position so the eye would see through the corrective portion. If he turned the lens, the prescription wouldn't match what was required. Every eye doctor in the world knew the principle.

Then the idea hit him—this simple fact could work to his advantage. Most lenses were made to fit the eye prescription, matching the particular patient's eye prescription with a specific corrective lens. But then he thought of it another way. He considered that the lens could be made in a generic system, perhaps. The lens could be designed to rotate to match the exact position the patient needed.

What if he could create a lens that could be twisted deliberately so that it would correct virtually any vision problem depending on the way it was oriented into the frame? He looked at the various eyeglass frames that surrounded him. An oval or rectangular fashion eyeglass wouldn't work, but a circular one would be ideal. If the frame and lens were round, it was entirely possible.

By this time, Jim Morrison was working in the eye care field, developing a business that would sell eyeglasses. He was interested in working with his father, and together Robert and Jim developed the new idea of a rotating lens that could be inserted into an inexpensive, round eyeglass frame.

As part of the introduction of the new product, they decided to launch Morrison International, an umbrella organization that would be privately held and dedicated to developing and marketing advanced, low cost eye care for underserved areas of the United States and developing countries.

Morrison International developed the system they called Morr-Sight. It not only worked with the principle of the rotating round lens, but included the method of diagnosing and disseminating the eyeglasses as well.

Robert planned to create an efficient and compact eye care office and laboratory that could be transported to the locations it was most needed. It would be a state-of-the-art eye care clinic and eyeglass dispensary that would be so compact in size that it could fit in a mobile lab installed in a bus or even in a small office anywhere in the world.

The mobile eye care units would each contain the full set of advanced vision equipment that would be easy to use. The equipment would include a special device that used infrared light to measure a person's vision and determine the corrective lenses required, plus standard equipment that could double-check the result. The mobile facility would also include the equipment to instantly make the eyeglasses on-site. Thus the patient would enter the mobile unit with a vision problem, and in most cases, would exit with the improved vision that had the potential to change his or her life.

The actual visual correction was based on a patented eyeglass design that would allow developing countries and impoverished areas to get eyeglasses on those in need. Robert and Jim experimented in making a round frame and a round lens that had a beveled edge which allowed the lens to pop right into 180 different positions or rotations of the optics. Each rotation would correct a different vision problem.

Robert originated the concept and worked on the optics while Jim invented the frame system. This would enable volunteers to assist in creating the eyeglasses to match the prescription.

The process would take just minutes. Since the software integrated the equipment and made the process simple, a technician could be trained to operate it with an optometrist or ophthalmologist supervising.

The Morr-Sight system could correct for astigmatism, myopia (nearsightedness), hyperopia (farsightedness), and presbyopia (a common condition in people over 40 who need a different prescription for distant vision and near vision). The system would also screen for glaucoma, a serious condition that, left untreated, is the leading cause of blindness in the world.

The vision prescription could be determined by an automated process, and a new manufacturing technique allowed them to make the lenses quickly. Each precision lens was properly centered in the frame according to the individual's inter-pupillary distance. Both the bridge and the temple of the unique frame could be adjusted to fit various facial structures, allowing it to be worn by men, women, or children. The simple, round, plastic frame and the single lens with its combined optical corrections could be manufactured at an inconceivably low price, one that would enable the poor of the world to see, to study, to work with a clear vision.

Most people with poor vision are myopic or nearsighted. With Jim and Robert's system, help was within reach for almost a quarter of the world's population. In India alone, the ramifications were immense. Hundreds of thousands of nearsighted people there were unable to function effectively. Students couldn't see the blackboard. Weavers were out of work.

The fact that these eyeglasses could improve someone's vision for just a dollar showed the staggering potential of the Morr-Sight sytem.

After eight years of development, using $300,000 of his own funds to begin Morr-Sight, Robert was able to supplement his efforts with fund-raising, eventually raising millions of dollars for Morr-Sight's efforts. The goal was to reach as many indigent people as possible by selling and leasing the Morr-Sight system to companies and governments. Investors would purchase the equipment and send it on the road via mobile laboratories in the United States and overseas. The mobile labs would be able to visit people in need wherever they were.

Robert approached Hershey Foods in nearby Hershey, Pennsylvania, with the idea of buying a bus they could donate for use in Africa, where the company gets its cocoa supplies. The company was interested but decided to first try the system out in the United States. Hershey Food's donated $500,000 to underwrite a Morr-Sight mobile eye clinic. The 18-month project that followed dispensed free eye care to schools, senior citizen facilities, migrant worker centers, blood banks, and other agencies in central Pennsylvania. The mobile clinic delivered not just free eye exams, but eyeglasses free of charge to the needy.

During the test run in Perry County, Pennsylvania, one of the state's poorest areas, hundreds of people went through the bus each day. Approximately 1,000 people left with prescription glasses. Some older people said they hadn't read in ten years due to poor vision.

Robert was still managing his own practice, but he volunteered on the mobile clinic. He found other volunteers and paid workers who examined eyes in various locations and provided frames and lenses on the spot.

The work was fulfilling. The very first day Robert worked on the mobile clinic, he was able to diagnose four cases of untreated glaucoma which he referred to local physicians. Since glaucoma can lead to blindness, the people who were diagnosed had essentially saved their vision.

The Rockefellers invested a million dollars in the effort, but though they called it an investment, they were more interested in doing good than considering it purely a business investment. Other investors included the Bronfman family, founders of Pep Boys automotive supply company, and the Gellman family, who owned fast food franchises in Canada. Robert Morrison's personal friends also added to the charity's finances.

Robert and Jim met with the World Health Organization in Geneva to inform the international group of the possibilities of providing affordable vision care. The WHO representative they met with at the time, Mrs. Bruggeman, noted that WHO was well aware of the challenge of improving vision in disadvantaged areas of the world.

Any solution that could help was extremely welcome and her enthusiasm conveyed itself in one statement. "It's one of the biggest problems and you've solved it."

Morr-Sight mobile clinics were able to travel as far as Brazil, where they provided eyeglasses for over 500 children. In the various areas it served, Morr-Sight eventually enabled 16,662 people to improve their vision through free exams and free eyeglasses.

Even those who weren't impoverished were able to enjoy some benefits due to the affordability of the Morr-Sight system. The Veterans Administration provided its veterans with a free prescription for their eyeglasses, but the cost of purchasing them would often result in the vets not filling their prescriptions. Morr-Sight offered to provide eyeglasses for the veterans at a cost of just $12. That amount easily covered Morr-Sight's costs, and the veterans could afford to purchase the eyeglasses; Morr-Sight was able to perform a service for America's vets and still run in the black.

Sadly, big business saw the prospect of affordable eyeglasses in another light. One of the Morr-Sight board members hired an MBA as a consultant, a man who was convinced that charity was not a business. He insisted that the company should be a regular optical business instead. They could charge more for the glasses and make an astounding profit. Robert insisted that the company was designed as something unique. It had been created to provide glasses for those who couldn't afford them. Unfortunately, to

Robert's great disappointment, the board favored the MBA, and the company eventually failed.

Jim Morrison opened a kiosk at a local mall to test the concept of selling eyeglasses affordably and creating them to order while people shopped. The prescription eyeglasses, although inexpensive because of the work of Jim and Robert, were precise and exact. People would bring their own prescription from their eye doctor, and the glasses would be created to the prescription. These glasses did not even have to be round since Jim had a bevel edger that could create a lens to fit the desired frame in under ten minutes.

Selling the glasses for $12 made a hefty profit while lowering the normal market price of glasses by hundreds of dollars. The mall kiosk was so popular that people stood in line to take advantage of the low cost.

# 19

## A CANCER CHALLENGE

I
N THE WINTER OF 2000, ROBERT MORRISON WAS 76 YEARS OLD.
He had slowed down, of course, but his energy and enthusiasm kept him young. He could have run rings around men ten or fifteen years his junior.

He and Ruth had begun to spend their winters in their Gulf-front condo on the island of Longboat Key just off Sarasota, Florida. They didn't want to leave their home in Harrisburg permanently, but in retirement—which to Robert simply meant working less but still teaching and consulting—the Northern winters seemed harder to endure. By this point in life, Robert had learned to slow down slightly and could consult from his condo which offered walks on the beach, sunny, warm weather, and views of the blue Gulf of Mexico from their balcony. It also meant quality time with their son, Jim, and their daughter, Patty, and their two families, who now both lived in Sarasota full time.

Tennis had always been a special pleasure in Robert's life. He loved the sport and thrived on the idea of competition, even if he was now in the senior leagues.

That year was no exception when it came to competition. Robert was enthusiastic about entering a local tennis tournament that was to be held near his Longboat Key home.

This particular tennis tournament was especially enjoyable. Robert's game seemed to be in exceptional form. His serve was on target, his forehand was strong, his lobs soared then landed on the baseline, and he passed his opponents down the line. His skill plus his persistence to hang in there on every point prevailed.

He won the tournament, thrilled as usual with the competition and happy that he was still able to win. True to old habits, however, he refused to boast. When asked about the match, he assumed the attitude that the other players had simply had an off-day, not that he'd played any better. He was just lucky, he guessed.

When the match was over, he felt ravenous, so he quickly showered and changed. He and Ruth had decided to meet at a near-by restaurant that was one of their special favorites for its food and atmosphere.

After they ordered, Robert let his excitement show with Ruth.

"I've never played that well," he said. "I think I may even play in the Nationals."

"That's a bit ambitious, Bobby." Ruth smiled, knowing that her husband would always try to find that extra challenge—even in his version of semiretirement.

"The Seniors, of course, for over 75's. I'm playing well."

"Then by all means, do it."

Ruth had learned that her Bobby thrived on challenge. She would support him just as he had always supported her throughout their 44 years of marriage.

Robert took another bite of his salad. It seemed to stick in his throat, but he chewed a bit more and managed to swallow. He didn't pay much attention to the problem. Just a particularly hard piece, perhaps. He drank some water to clear the passageway, but as he continued to eat, he realized that each bite seemed difficult to swallow. He had never noticed that problem before.

He felt his neck. Strange ... there was a lump there, just at the base of his throat.

"What's the matter?" Ruth leaned forward to see what he was doing.

"It seems like a lump, right here." He used his index finger to touch the area. "I think the gland is swollen."

"Could you be coming down with something? Is your throat sore?"

"No. It's not a cold."

"Let me see." Ruth leaned across the table and moved Bobby's hand away from his throat and felt the lump herself.

"That's not where the kids got swollen glands."

"Well, it's probably nothing."

"Probably not," Ruth agreed, but her eyes were concerned. "You should see a doctor about it."

"I'm so busy, Ruthie."

It wasn't often Ruth would insist on anything. This time she did.

"See a doctor, Bobby. Soon."

The very next day Robert saw their family doctor in Sarasota, Dr. Randy Silverstine. He felt the lump and asked Robert some questions, but Dr. Silverstine was an internist. He had his suppositions, but this wasn't his specialty, so he told Robert that it would be best if he were to get an immediate appointment with someone who had special expertise in throat problems. Dr. Silverstine recommended an ear, nose, and throat specialist that he knew in the area, Dr. Dan Deems.

That same day, Dr. Deems examined Robert's throat and felt the dime-sized lump. He had seen this problem before, so even though his expression was professional, it seemed grave.

"I think we should do a biopsy."

"Biopsy?" Robert guessed the answer but he was hoping he was wrong. "Why?"

He looked at Robert. "No use in worrying too soon, but we do have to consider a possible cancer. Hopefully, we'll just rule it out, but we need the biopsy."

"No one in my family has cancer. I doubt that's what it is."

Robert had boundless optimism and had always been in excellent health. Nevertheless, a nervous flutter hit his stomach. The doctor had used the word he wanted to ignore. Of course, everyone may think occasionally about such things as cancer ... but him? He was the guy who ate a healthy diet, didn't smoke, and had always been active and exercised—and he'd just won a tennis tournament, for heaven's sake!

Later, Robert found out that Dr. Deems, who'd done the biopsy, had received the results and they were definitive. Because the Morrisons were planning to return to Harrisburg soon, Dr. Deems thought it best that the Morrisons connect with a physician in Robert's hometown who would be able to make treatment recommendations and provide the follow-up care that would be needed.

He recommended that Robert see an excellent specialist near Harrisburg named Dr. Randall Weber at the University of Pennsylvania. It was Dr. Weber, a specialist in treating throat cancer, who pronounced the dreaded words.

The cancer was in a lymph node. It was a bad sign. Cancer never begins in a lymph node itself, and this diagnosis meant the cancer had begun in another area. Normally, cancer travels from another location in the body and lodges in the lymph nodes. It was necessary to find the primary site, and to do so, Dr. Weber would have to operate.

Dr. Weber performed what is called a modified radical neck dissection, which discovered a squamous cell cancer located at the base of Robert's tongue. From there, the cancer cells had spread to the nearby lymph node.

To eliminate the cancer, two choices were available. The first would involved cutting off a piece of Robert's tongue, but in that case, he would have to live with a speech defect the rest of his life. The second choice was radiation therapy, which had often proven to be effective on squamous cell cancer. It meant taking a chance that the radiation would be effective in this case, but if it worked, Robert's ability to speak could be salvaged.

For a man who had made a career of lecturing throughout the world, instructing fellow professionals and patients, with a love of speech in all its forms, the first choice was not an acceptable solution.

Radiation followed. A lot of it. For 35 days, Robert would have to return every day to be treated at the University of Pennsylvania Department of Radiation in Philadelphia.

Robert and Ruth stayed at Robert's aunt's apartment in Rittenhouse Square in one of Philadelphia's pleasantest suburbs. Robert's aunt, Sophy Curson, who was known for her elegant dress shop in Philadelphia, had fallen, and was temporarily in a rehabilitation facility. She'd gladly made her apartment available to Robert and Ruth.

It was a difficult time. Each day, Robert and Ruth took a taxi to the University of Pennsylvania Department of Radiation where Robert underwent treatment. Though the radiation therapy wasn't painful in and of itself, the side effects took their toll. Robert suffered from nausea that often accompanies radiation therapy, and at times, he could hardly keep his head up. Though he remained in relatively good spirits, for once in his life Robert lost his inexhaustible energy.

The cancer was beaten. Robert was pronounced cancer-free in May 2000. The radiation battle, however, had left a side effect that would forever change Robert's lifestyle. In destroying the cancer, the radiation therapy had also destroyed the salivary glands which are essential in moistening the mouth for speaking and eating.

From then on, Robert's mouth would be constantly dry, and he would need to apply special lubrication in order to speak well.

In addition, normal eating habits were not possible. Robert could only take fluids.

He called on his natural optimism. As he said, "I'm lucky enough to have modern medicine kill the cancer cells even if they did have an adverse effect. I am fine and feel fortunate."

He continued to join Ruth for special dinners, but the man who had dined in palaces, celebrity homes, and the world's finest restaurants could not eat solid foods. He dined on the liquid meal, Ensure.

# 20

## SLOWING DOWN
## BUT NOT RETIRING

B EACH WALKS AND TENNIS GAMES HAD TAKEN A BACKSEAT while Robert fought cancer. Fortunately, he did win the battle. The prognosis was now excellent he would live and enjoy life with the same enthusiasm he'd always shown. He would continue to consult on eye care and to play tennis. He would become involved in social life with Ruth at their homes in Harrisburg and Longboat Key in Florida. He'd continue to travel and visit many of the royals and celebrities who he'd known as patients and friends.

He just wouldn't be sharing gourmet meals at royal palaces or elegant New York restaurants. The radiation had, as he told a friend, "fried my salivary glands." His mouth was always dry, and he could only swallow liquid nourishment.

Despite that setback, he continued to work and share his expertise. At 80 years of age, Dr. Robert Morrison was still being called upon for his specialized advice. His counsel was usually sought due to unusual problems or a combination of vision complications. Robert was the expert when it came to tackling situations that others would trouble over. Somehow, he often managed to come up with a solution or combination of solutions that would help.

The calls often involved interesting cases, and if Robert could help, he was always glad to provide his expertise. If he felt he couldn't, he would often phone others more knowledgeable or urge the caller to contact a specialist he could recommend.

One day, it was a phone call from halfway around the world. A representative of the Lions Club in Bombay, India, needed advice on possible ways to improve the vision of a teenager who was albino, lacking normal pigmentation in his skin. Because the boy lacked normal pigmentation in his eyes as well, he was extremely sensitive to light—a condition known as photophobia. The 15-year-old's father had an automobile repair business but couldn't afford the specialized care which he could receive in the United States.

The Lions Club was willing to help the boy financially if Dr. Morrison could help his eyes. Thanks to the Lions Club, the boy eventually was able to visit the United States, and Robert took on the case.

He discovered that the boy not only had photophobia, but also nystagmus, the same constant movement of the eye that he treated successfully for other patients. To counteract light sensitivity, Robert prescribed tinted contact lenses that would lessen the amount of light entering the eye. He also prescribed low vision devices, and when the boy returned home, he was finally able to read and see television.

By coincidence, Robert was later asked to consult on another situation in which a younger boy, also albino and lacking pigmentation, not only had photophobia but also ataxia, a problem in muscle coordination. Robert consulted with the attending doctor and suggested that tinted contact lenses might help. However, if the iris sphincter did not respond to light, then he'd recommend a good neurologist who could try to discover the cause of the conditions.

Robert didn't believe in merely treating the symptom. "Treatment alone is not enough. It's best when the cause is uncovered."

His thoroughness was one reason for his success, so the calls for advice continue. Like his career, they span the globe.


HER MAJESTY QUEEN JULIANA DIED IN 2004, AND PRINCE BERNHARD died several months afterwards at age 93. More than just patients, they had become Robert's friends. Prince Albert of Monaco knew of their special friendships, and it was he who called to tell Robert the sad news each time, suggesting that Robert might want to accompany him to the funerals.

When Prince Rainier of Monaco passed away in 2005, it was the youthful Prince Albert—for whom Robert had once prescribed contact lenses—who was to become the new leader of Monaco. Robert and Ruth, as longtime friends, were invited to attend the Investiture. They were the only Americans invited. The ceremony was filled with royals who'd been Robert's patients and were now his friends.


ROBERT STILL HAS ALL THOSE GREAT MEMORIES. AND THE ROLLS ... it sits, as gleaming as the day it first arrived at Baltimore Harbor, in the underground garage of his condominium, not covered with a tarp like the Porsche next to it, but easy and elegant, gassed up and ready to drive like any practical car you might own. Like its owner, it has a humble attitude, a sense of its worth and sophistication, but without false pretense.

A host of other anomalies are woven throughout Robert Morrison's life. Many people have called him a genius, but he never considered himself a towering intellectual, and he himself always considered his brother Victor as the better student. Nor did he consider his oratory particularly dazzling. It only became impressive when he began discussing ophthalmological or optometric materials and techniques. Then the terms relating to his specialty, whether dealing with the chemistry of contact lens materials or corrections for corneal malfunctions, drifted out naturally from a man to whom it became second nature to consider the most technologically advanced and innovative means to improving vision.

He was not a master entrepreneur or even good at business. He left the practical details to specialists. He never had the ruthless drive to make money; in fact, a basic trust in the wrong people lost him much of the profit from his inventions. Yet he ran a successful private practice and presided over various corporations that were to make him a multimillionaire.

His accomplishments did not come about as a goal in themselves. Robert Morrison never set out to earn riches or fame. It happened because he simply set out to become the best he could be in his chosen field.

Today, Dr. Robert Morrison is taking the Rolls-Royce for a spin around St. Armands Circle, the posh shopping area just a mile down the road from his Longboat Key condo. The Rolls has a Florida license plate, so he doesn't have to be concerned about the policeman directing traffic at one of the intersections. He won't be stopped except by admiring glances. A tourist calls out, asking how old the Rolls is and Robert answers simply. "1961."

Little do they know how far in life that car and its driver have traveled.

# 21

## A Conversation
## With Dr. Morrison

THROUGH STUDY, ENTHUSIASM, TALENT, AND CREATIVE THINKING, Dr. Robert Morrison has achieved amazing success. By helping to develop the soft contact lens, he helped millions to enjoy better vision more comfortably. His unique solutions to vision problems helped patients from royalty to the disadvantaged to see better, enhancing their quality of life.

The man himself is a wonderful example of humanity, with his professional and personal goals being the same—to simply do the best he can. We spoke with him to discuss his life and philosophy.

## On Doing a Book About Your Life

*Q: We learned that many authors asked you about writing a book and you always declined. Why did you finally decide to go ahead with a book?*

A: Two of my dearest friends, Harry Pincus and Bill Saunders, urged me and convinced me to do this. Harry Pincus is a lawyer from Norfolk, Virginia. Bill Saunders, formerly from California and now retired but still consulting, lives in Monaco. They insisted that I owe it to my grandchildren to let them know some of my feelings and occurrences. They urged me to sit down with some good writers and complete this task.

## On Learning

*Q: How important do you think degrees are?*

A: Research shows the original doctorate was a Ph.D., but now we have the M.D., D.O., D.P.M., O.D., Ed.D., D.M.D., D.D., J.D., etc. In many countries in Europe the completion of law school makes you a notary and advanced work in a graduate school gives you a doctorate. I have found all graduate schools are fine schools and graduate well-educated people. Some go on to serve mankind well, some less so. My opinion is—continue to learn and get better in whatever field you chose and do your very best for every individual who seeks your care or guidance.

*Q: If you had life to do all over again, what would you do differently?*

A: Study more. Be a better and more dedicated student.

*Q: Many people consider you to be self-deprecating. Do you ever feel inadequate?*

A: Yes and often. But if I need to know something to help a patient, I either study the pertinent material or seek someone who has the expertise in the area of need.

*Q: You're so interested in learning. Is there any technical area that frustrates you?*

A: The awesome computer! It fascinates me but I have little knowledge of how it works or how to use it.

## On Developing the Soft Contact Lens

*Q: You claim that Professor Wichterle was the true genius in creating the HEMA gel you worked with. Why is that?*

A: Professor Wichterle and Dr. Lim invented the hydrophilic gel (HEMA) and that was the major breakthrough. I just constantly sought some better material to make contact lenses. The fact that I spent many hours with Professor Wichterle and he sought knowledge of optics from me was not so special. Many optometrists or ophthalmologists who knew optics, and many do, could have done what I did just as well, perhaps better.

*Q: You seemed to admire Professor Wichterle (deceased) a great deal.*

A: Indeed, I did respect him, and I do not like to mention other opinions which may or may not be true.

*Q: That's really not an adequate answer. What other opinions are you referring to?*

A: OK! This is not my opinion ... some Czechs seemed to feel he was both egotistical and opportunistic, not really caring who got hurt along the way. Some feel he pushed Dr. Lim—the co-patent holder with Professor Wichterle—out. Some feel his getting into bed with Pollock and Feldman against me was a terrible, even an inexcusable decision. Professor Wichterle continued working with those two even after their unethical advancement on me. Some Czechs did not like that association at all. They still look down on it.

*Q: Do you agree even partially with some of these sentiments?*

A: I really do not care to comment.

*Q: Did you ever hear from Dr. Lim again?*

A: Yes, in fact we met each other at a meeting of CLAO (Contact Lens Association of Ophthalmologists, Inc.). Dr. Lim and I were both invited to speak.

*Q: What did Dr. Lim say?*

A: In his remarks to everyone at the meeting, he said that Wichterle and he did many experiments during their work in the chemistry laboratories, developed many interesting products. Some were patented and some were not. He also said, "Make no bones about it, Dr. Robert Morrison brought the soft contact lens to the world and now 50 million people wear them." He added, "Without Morrison's wisdom, drive, and belief in the hydrophilic gel, the soft contact lens may have gone the way of many of our other developments that never left the chemistry lab."

*Q: Do you know whatever happened to Dr. Lim?*

A: Dr. Lim left Czechoslovakia and settled in San Diego, California, working for Revlon. I've been told he died in San Diego.

# On Contact Lens Wear

*Q: How do you feel about allergies and wearing contact lenses?*

A: Some excellent new preparations work against allergies and have helped many to wear contact lenses who might otherwise not be able to. However, when nothing helps, it is best to wear eyeglasses and not use contact lenses until the response subsides.

*Q: Do you wear contact lenses yourself?*

A: I have excellent distant vision but need some help at near. When I lecture, I usually put a contact lens on my non-dominant eye so I can see my notes. When at home and no one is looking, I put on a pair of glasses for prolonged near vision. This allows the use of two eyes.

There are bifocal lenses, and at the time of this writing, the rigid ones are excellent, though they require some skill in prescribing and fitting. The soft bifocals are fairly good. They're fine for shopping and reading a price tag, but are not good for prolonged tasks requiring close-up work such as sewing or reading a book.

*Q: How do you feel about sleeping with contact lenses on the eye?*

A: If there is no edema (swelling of the cornea) and if the lens is clean (some lenses accumulate mucus, protein deposits, and other unwanted deposits), I think sleeping with contact lenses is OK. The FDA recently approved a lens that is part silicone to be worn 30 days. If there is edema in greater amounts than normally noted, I do not recommend wearing the lenses even one night. If the lens is clean and there's no edema problem, more than 30 days is OK.

## On New Vision Technologies

*Q: How do you feel about orthokeratology?*

A: *Ortho* is Greek for straight, and *keratology* refers to the cornea. Some optometrists believe strongly that refractive errors can be eliminated or lessened by wearing special contact lenses. Some recommend wearing them at night. I have never been attracted to this interesting field as I like to change the cornea as little as possible. There are some very clever and dedicated practitioners who have achieved excellent results.

*Q: Do you approve of the new laser surgery?*

A: Sort of like the old nursery rhyme—when it is good, it is very very good. I read an article, I think it was by Brian Holden, Ph.D., that said that one in every 14 people interviewed were sorry they had the procedure done. My experience was that I met many of the thirteen satisfied patients who were very happy, but ...

*Q: What is the but?*

A: We do not know the long term effects of operating on healthy eyes. Maybe glaucoma some day, maybe some other problem, like corneal decompensation. Maybe no side effects or even healthier eyes? Who knows? We do know that all surgery is not reversible. If contact lenses are poorly fitted and not wearable, you can take them off and wear glasses or have the contact lenses refitted. The eye has not been altered surgically.

*Q: What are some of the problems with laser surgery?*

A: Dry eyes, flare at night which causes difficulty in night driving. Generally the surgery is considered cosmetic and may be costly.

## On Celebrity

*Q: I heard people and doctors came to see you from all over the world. How did you feel about this?*

A: Flattered.

*Q: Was your goal ever fame or fortune?*

A: I know it was not fortune. I do also know that my office manager's concern for fiscals allowed me not to have to be involved. I just don't know if I would have been more concerned if she wasn't. It might sound corny, but I always knew the financial affairs were OK, and I could afford to be involved in other pursuits.

*Q: How do you feel when caring for royalty?*

A: They are human beings. OK, it is great fun and very flattering to touch the lives of the royal families, but the eye care is the same.

*Q: How about the celebrities? Movie stars?*

A: Same. They are human beings and deserve the same special care that everyone deserves. Sure it is fun and flattering, but they are the special ones, not the one giving the care.

*Q: What was it like to work with so many celebrities?*

A: It would not be truthful to say that I was not thrilled and delighted when they called upon me. I think I was honored and pleased, but I really did my best for everyone regardless of their position or achievements.

*Q: Why do you think you succeeded?*

A: I don't feel I have succeeded. I do confess to trying very hard to do my best at whatever I do. Perhaps not concentrating on money but on projects was a help. I could say that knowing when to abandon a project is worthwhile, but I think I persisted longer on some projects than I should have.

*Q: Many psychiatrists and psychologists feel strongly that one must love oneself. How do you feel about that?*

A: I'm sure they know much more about human behavior that I do, but I disagree. I believe it is of real personal value to seek excellence in one's chosen field. If self-esteem ensues, I am OK with that.

*Q: How did you handle mentally all the magazine and newspaper articles about you?*

A: I think public relations is far better than it ought to be. People came to see me from very faraway places because they read something about me. Everyone seems to know what makes a good story; facts are not as important as they should be and exaggeration is not uncommon.

## On Professional Life

*Q: How do you feel about ophthalmologists and optometrists advertising?*

A: I try hard not to be judgmental, but deep down I really do not like it. I feel we have little enough time to think, perhaps when we're driving a car. I would rather think of one patient, one idea to work on, than a clever ad to be on TV, radio, billboards, etc. I truly feel each must do what he feels is best and conducting myself as best I can is my responsibility. Others have different thoughts and that is OK with me.

*Q: Does advertising work in the eye care field?*

A: I think so. I have no experience, but one that advertises glaucoma care sees a lot more patients with glaucoma than others who do not promote this type of care. One who promotes sports vision sees more athletes. I think it does work but I do feel that good care by a caring person also works and I prefer that modality.

*Q: Does location help an eye care practice?*

A: I think not. Peggy loved to use the computer and compiled all kinds of statistics. Over half my patients traveled more than 50 miles to see me—or perhaps the locals knew better!

*Q: Do you think being born in Harrisburg was helpful? You had a base of friends there when you began your practice.*

A: I really don't think so. My friends didn't immediately seek eye care from me. I really did not blame them. Why go to a young, new guy when so many older and more experienced practitioners were around? It was years before any friends came to me for eye care.

*Q: Your colleagues tell me one of your more interesting lectures was given at the University of California. Tell us about it.*

A: A wonderful researcher and clinician, Dr. Mort Saver, had died. The School of Optometry there decided to memorialize him with a program and invited me to speak on corneal physiology. They changed their minds and gave me the task of speaking on practice management. I was a bit disappointed, but I did deliver the lecture and was surprised to learn how many seemed to enjoy it and asked for reprints.

*Q: Why was that? What did you say?*

A: I felt there were three important points. First, be a good practitioner—read, study, attend lectures, go wherever the opportunity to learn might be. Second, be a nice person—be genuinely interested in whatever is said. Look into the eye, listen carefully. Be kind and considerate to all in the office or out. Third, be perceived as such. A doctor can be excellent and not pleasant or vice versa. But if the doctor has knowledge, is a nice person, and the patient or public sees him or her as both knowledgeable and nice, then a large practice will not only ensue, but self-respect accompanies it.

*Q: Were you paid well for your lectures?*

A: I know it may be difficult to believe, but I never thought much about it. I tried to accept every invitation to speak I received. I left Peggy to handle my schedule, travel arrangements, and speaking fees. After awhile she quoted $1,000 per lecture, and later when the popularity thing was booming, she changed it to $5,000, but she never spoke to me about it. Sometimes the fee went to charity. In the case of the talk mentioned at the University of California, she quoted the then usual $5,000. All the speakers, however, spoke without remuneration and, of course, so did I. We did each receive a sweatshirt that said *University of California*!

*Q: It's difficult to believe you did so well financially and were unaware of this.*

A: I knew the lectures I did were well attended and profitable. I knew the practice in Harrisburg, Pennsylvania, and the one on Park Avenue in New York City were very busy, booked weeks ahead. I knew I had no financial worries, and my wife did not like to spend. So I knew all was OK financially, but I did not think about it. I was lucky that I could think of other projects and had an excellent assistant.

*Q: Your offices in Harrisburg and in New York City were beautiful and you worked in palaces all over the world. Were luxurious surroundings important to you?*

A: I never thought about it from a personal view, but it was certainly nice to work in a pleasant environment and with the very best equipment. I do think my staff and my patients enjoyed the environment.

*Q: Did you have some ideas that did not succeed?*

A: Yes. I pursued many projects and they certainly were not all good ones. For example, I patented a device that would accurately measure a corneal lesion so that the practitioner could tell whether a treatment or time had effected a change. I was pretty proud and excited about it, but it never seemed to move the practitioners.

## On His Personal Life

*Q: Was your wife a factor in your achieving so much?*

A: Oh, yes. She did think I was a bit overactive, but at no time did she ever say—why are you going there? Why? She just supported me with pride in whatever I pursued, regardless of how absurd she may have thought the project to be.

*Q: Do you have a story or two involving your wife you'd like to share?*

A: Yes ... here's one. Some years ago I was asked to lecture in Taipei, Taiwan, and Ruthie joined me. When we arrived at the hotel, we were given a tremendous welcome, and each night we were treated to a different type of fine restaurant. Well, one night, I casually mentioned that it was Ruthie's birthday the next day. They picked us up the next day, took us to some elegant restaurant, and while Ruthie and I were sitting in the backseat of the car as it pulled up to some elegant Cantonese restaurant, a machine gun *rat a tat tat* began! I threw Ruthie to the floor, and jumped on top of her to protect her ... only to learn that it was just fireworks they'd set off to celebrate her birthday!

*Q: Do you have another one?*

A: Yes. ... I was at the Chamber of Commerce receiving an award. The governor of Pennsylvania gave me a plaque and I was called on to speak. I said very little, thanked my parents who were there as guests, and said thank-you to my wife for putting up with all my unreasonable energies. The governor said, "Let's see the woman who puts up with these unreasonable energies." Ruthie waved a hi, and the governor said, "Oh, no, please stand up so we can all see what a woman looks like that puts up with unreasonable energy." Ruthie was in her last month—maybe last days of pregnancy—and she stood up so all around could see this round and wonderful girl ... it was too funny!

*Q: It sounds like you've made life interesting for Ruth. Why do you often call her Ruthie?*

A: My older brother, Alan, also married a Ruth, and she is Ruth Morrison. Also, my Ruthie was called Ruthie all her life by her parents and her brother. By the way, he died last year. He was a prisoner of war, shot down on his first flight from England to Germany. A German family turned him in, and he, Leonard Rapoport, was eventually freed by the Russians.

*Q: I've heard you have some difficulty getting to where you're supposed to be going when you're driving.*

A: Ruthie always says my mind is just not where we are going, and we often get lost by taking the wrong road. One time I picked up a doctor from South Africa named Benny Mirkin at the Kennedy Airport in New York. We were driving, and after awhile he said, "This is my first trip to America but I have been studying maps and would like to ask you most respectfully, does one go through Connecticut to get to Pennsylvania?" I told him, "No, it is in the opposite direction." He said, "We are in Connecticut." We were, and I made a U-turn and drove home.

*Q: Do you think your achievements made life more difficult for your two children?*

A: I hope not. I really care a great deal about both of them and think I would do anything to make life better for them. My wife is a strong believer in allowing everyone to reach their individual potential.

*Q: You have a sister and two brothers. Are you close?*

A: Definitely. I could not ask for better or more supportive brothers, and my sister seems to think anything her three brothers do is great. Our parents taught us to accept the other three with love and respect, even if we did not agree with their pursuits.

*Q: What about friendships?*

A: My mother taught us that family and good friends are the very best things in life. I think I have learned to value these relationships.

*Q: What was the highlight of your life?*

A: I really think having a nice wife, two wonderful children, and five grandchildren is as good as one can ever dream of.

*Q: You have such a pleasant disposition. What do you attribute that to?*

A: My wife. I have a very nice and happy home life.

*Q: I have learned that you have always been that way, long before you met your wife.*

A: Probably naiveté. I once read that Will Rogers said, "I never met a man I didn't like." I borrow that but add to it. "I never met a man or woman I didn't like."

*Q: What about people who are rude or abrasive? There are some, you know.*

A: I prefer to think those people are having a bad day, perhaps a bad period of time, perhaps some less than desirable thinking. I am sure some of this silly feeling is part of my determination to think everyone is OK, which is why I call it naiveté.

*Q: You have two brothers and speak well of both of them. Your younger brother, Victor, was also an optometrist. Any sibling rivalry there?*

A: I don't think so. Victor is very bright and I always thought he was much brighter than I was, and he has strong opinions. He did very well in Mechanicsburg, Pennsylvania. When I saw things were going so well, I asked him to join me in my practice, but he was doing great and decided not to.

## On Religion

*Q: You've treated people of all races and religions equally. Does your religion play a strong role in your life?*

A: I want to believe in God, a force, something. I cite the human body in its many marvels as a wonder and I always give an example from the eye—the tear gland, the tear duct, the action of the eyelids, gravity, the absence of blood vessels in the cornea—it all comes together to allow us to see.

I'm constantly puzzled, though, about why we accept ideas that have never been proven, often not even recorded for hundreds of years? Maybe because they are so beautiful and wholesome, maybe we just need something to hold onto. I like to quote the King of Siam when he wondered about many things and said, "Is a puzzlement." I say, if there is a God, and I hope there is, I will not be punished for being inquisitive, questioning, or puzzled.

*Q: Does it play out in your daily life?*

A: My wonderful mother used to say, "never discuss religion or politics with anyone except if they are intelligent. Then you will find these two topics the most interesting possible." Perhaps she should have said open-minded and intelligent. As I said, the beautiful thoughts of a soul, or afterlife, are ideas that are so attractive, yet man-made and warmly passed on through generations. They all puzzle me. But I truly do believe in leading a good, clean life, doing some good for others, making the world a bit better because I was here.

## On Current International Affairs

*Q: It has been reported that you sent some comments to both the current Secretary of Homeland Security, Michael Chertoff, and his predecessor, Tom Ridge. Did you?*

A: Yes, but only suggestions. They know so much more than I do, but I did share some of my thoughts.

*Q: What exactly were they?*

A: I suggested three things. Please remember they were only suggestions. First, I read where they planned to use iris scanning at airports, etc., as it was quicker and not as messy as fingerprinting. I reported that there was an eye drop often used for glaucoma therapy that changed the color of the iris. If coloration is part of the iris scan technique, it could be a problem. Second, I noted that the anthrax powder that has already killed some innocent people has been transported in envelopes. I thought some messages and greeting cards might be used in a post card format, avoiding the use of envelopes completely. My third suggestion involved the so-called black box that the media refers to whenever there's an airplane crash. I mentioned the fact that if the box was fluorescent orange instead of black, the searchers might be able to use a flashlight with a cobalt blue filter over the light source which would make the box fluoresce and be much easier to find. We actually use this in contact lens fitting and, of course, hunters wear clothes that fluoresce so they are easily spotted and less apt to be shot at by other hunters.

*Q: My research indicates the iris program you've referred to has been abandoned and a new program using the retina instead is being studied and looks promising. I've also learned that the black box is no longer black but orange as you suggested. I heard that mentioned during the recent airplane disaster in Kentucky. It might feel good for you to know that both of those changes came about as the result of your efforts. Have you any other ideas about such things as international affairs?*

A: Again, I remind you, I am not trained or skilled in these areas. I have been lucky to travel a lot and have noticed something very difficult in recent years. Not too many years ago, when I said I was from the United States, I heard nothing but wonderful comments about our great country, its freedom, etc. Recently, I have found the opposite. Many people I have chatted with throughout the world seem to think the very worst about our country, in spite of the fact that we in the USA are not the least bit interested or desirous in conquering anyone. We just want all people to be free and we have the most pleasant wishes for all. I think we need an enormous, truthful, effective public relations campaign to tell the people of the world that this great country wants only the best for everyone. I don't feel, based on the many foreigners I have spoken to, that our goals and desires are understood.

*Q: I heard you were actually invited to join some prominent Americans at the War College for a week involving exchanging ideas.*

A: I've had that privilege a few times and I think it was one of the biggest honors anyone could possibly have.

*Q: Do you have any particular memories about the experience?*

A: At one point someone, I think it was the Secretary of Defense, said, "Dr. Morrison, you have a puzzled look on your face. Please tell us what you're thinking." I said, "Sir, we are products of the media. We know what the newspapers, television, radio, magazines, etc. tell us. You fine minds in Washington know much more than we do as we are so limited in what we learn. Your judgments are made after learning facts we don't and perhaps shouldn't know. I am honored to be here, but I think my opinions are not based on the same facts you have and I wonder why I am even here."

## On Sports

*Q: How good a tennis player were, or are, you?*

A: Medium rare. I played number one on my high school and college teams, won a lot of not important tennis tournaments and lots

of doubles including a state championship, but I had a good partner. I won lots of mixed doubles tournaments—liked playing with
girls! But my two brothers, Alan and Vic, were both better tennis
players than I was, as well as very nice guys. My older brother,
Alan, was fascinated with tennis, read books, etc. He had a lot to
do with Vic and I liking the game. He stimulated us in many ways.
My younger brother, Vic, also stimulated me in many ways, he
always did everything well, I didn't.

*Q: What motivated you to be a better tennis player?*

A: I read an article in high school that said—be careful of your
ego; all athletes think they are better than they really are. I wanted
to be careful. I fought very hard to win every point, but when I lost
(too often), I wanted to be a good loser and a good sport.

*Q: Tennis is your first love, but what about other sports?*

A: If I could add on to the end of my life all the hours I spent playing sports, I would live to be a very old man. I liked baseball and
football. My specialty in baseball was flying out to the outfield.
I seemed to hit the ball into the outfield, often high and caught.
Football? I weighed 125 pounds, and a good breeze would blow
me over. I did love to tackle a bigger guy and thought I was pretty
tough when I did. Spent thousands of hours playing basketball at
what we called the Grubmeyer Athletic Club, an alley behind my
friend Charley Grubmeyer's house.

## On His Life's Work

*Q: If you had it to do all over again, would you be an optometrist?*

A: I would. I wanted to do something in health care. I did not want to operate nor deal with terrible diseases, life or death. But I greatly respect and admire those who do.

*Q: I have no other questions. Do you have anything you'd like to add or expound on?*

A: You have made me sound so good. I really don't feel that good, and I wonder about all the kind praise. I did, and I do, try very hard and love to do and say nice things—and love to do them well, but...

*Q: But what?*

A: I truly do not feel special. I am fortunate and nice things have happened to me. But others are possibly more skilled but not so lucky.

# ACKNOWLEDGMENTS

Learning is a lifetime process. I would like to acknowledge with gratitude those who have taught me about eyes, contact lenses, and related matters, most especially the care of patients who have entrusted themselves to me. I am certain that I've learned much from the following:

Dr. Ali Aminlari, Pennsylvania
Dr. Neal Bailey, Ohio
Mr. Gregory Band, Florida
Dr. Stanley Bank, Pennsylvania
Dr. Kenneth Barrisch, New York
Mr. Norman Bier, England
Dr. George Blankenship, Pennsylvania
Professor Roger Bonnet, France
Dr. Irving Borisch, Indiana
Dr. Milton Braveman, Pennsylvania
Dr. L. O. Brenner, Pennsylvania
Dr. Thomas Brungardt, Kansas
Dr. Richard Buckius, Pennsylvania
Dr. Gilberto Cepero, Cuba
Dr. Eduordo Cerulli, Pennsylvania
Dr. Kathy Clark, Pennsylvania
Dr. I. William Collins, Pennsylvania
Dr. William Cooley, Massachusetts
Dr. Bill Cosby, New York
Dr. Chris Covert, Pennsylvania
Dr. Edward Dailey, Pennsylvania
Dr. Harold Davis, Illinois
Mr. John DeCarle, England

Dr. Daniel Deems, Florida
Dr. Robert Denison, Pennsylvania
Mr. Frank Dickinson, England
Dr. Maximillan Dreyfus, Switzerland
Dr. Michael Dunn, New York
Dr. Andrew Eller, Pennsylvania
Mr. Melvin Eller, Pennsylvania
Dr. Peter Eller, Rhode Island
Dr. Ihor Fedoriw, Pennsylvania
Mr. Colin Field, South Africa
Mr. Richard Fox, Pennsylvania
Dr. Donald Freedman, Pennsylvania
Mr. Harry Freeman, England
Dr. Michael Friedberg, Pennsylvania
Mrs. Ragnhild Futerman, England
Dr. Miles Galin, New York
Mr. Jeffrey Galley, England
Dr. Thomas Gardner, Pennsylvania
Dr. Antonio Gasset, Florida
Dr. Joseph Goldberg, Virginia
Dr. Stanley Gordon, New York
Mr. Charles Grubmeyer, Pennsylvania
Dr. Theo Gumpelmayer, Austria

Dr. Istvan Gyoffrey, Hungary
Mr. Francis B. Haas, Jr., Pennsylvania
Dr. Edward Hackenbrack, Pennsylvania
Dr. Sami El Hage, Lebanon
Dr. Jack Hartstein, Missouri
Dr. Richard Hill, Ohio
Mr. Fred Hodd, England
Dr. Lawrence Hurwitz, Florida
Dr. Lester Janoff, Pennsylvania
Dr. George Jessen, Nevada
Dr. Joshua Josephson, Canada
Dr. Jan Jurkus, Illinois
Dr. Hyman Kahn, Pennsylvania
Dr. Harry Kaplan, Pennsylvania
Dr. Karl Kaufman, Pennsylvania
Dr. Richard Keates, Ohio
Dr. Charles Kelman, New York
Dr. Hermann Kemmetmueller, Austria
Mr. Bernard Kemp, England
Dr. Robert Koetting, Missouri
Dr. Elwood Kolb, Pennsylvania
Dr. Donald Korb, Massachusetts
Dr. H. Kornbluth, Israel
Dr. Minster Kunkle, Pennsylvania
Dr. Peter Laibson, Pennsylvania
Ms. Anette Leask, Pennsylvania
Dr. Alan Lenig, Indiana
Mr. Edwin Levey, South Africa
Dr. Levinson, Israel
Dr. Thomas Lewis, Pennsylvania
Dr. David Liang, Pennsylvania
Mr. Ted Lick, Pennsylvania
Dr. Loh, Singapore
Dr. Robert Lookabough, Nebraska
Dr. Robert Mandell, California
Dr. Kenneth Messner, Pennsylvania
Dr. David Miller, Massachusetts
Dr. Bruce Miller, Pennsylvania
Dr. Lin Moore, Oklahoma
Mr. Alan Morrison, Pennsylvania
Dr. Jeffrey Morrison, Pennsylvania
Dr. Victor Morrison, Pennsylvania
Dr. Tonia Mortelliti, New York
Dr. Robert Munsch, Missouri
Dr. John C. Neill, Pennsylvania
Dr. Helena Orlova, Russia

Dr. Maurice Osher, Ohio
Ms. Marilyn Oskie, Pennsylvania
Dr. Mohammed Ousqui, Iran
Mr. Harry Pincus, Virginia
Dr. William Policoff, Pennsylvania
Dr. Kenneth Polse, California
Dr. Maurice Poster, New York
Dr. Donald Praeger, New York
Dr. David Quillen, Pennsylvania
Mrs. Harriet Raffel
Dr. Randolph, Texas
Dr. Melvin Remba, California
Dr. R. Robbins, New York
Mr. Pierre Rocher, France
Mr. Edward Rosen, Pennsylvania
Ms. Yvonne Rosenberger, Pennsylvania
Dr. Alfred Rosenbloom, Illinois
Dr. Perry Rosenthal, Massachusetts
Dr. M. Rubin, England
Mr. Robert Sabel, New York
Dr. Morton Sarver, California
Dr. Joseph Sassoni, Pennsylvania
Virginia and Bill Saunders, Monaco
Dr. Charles Schick, Indiana
Dr. Robert Schwartz, Pennsylvania
Dr. Richard Shugarman, Florida
Dr. Randy Silverstine, Florida
Mr. James Smeltzer, Pennsylvania
Dr. Richard Smith, New York
Mr. Peter Sohnges, Germany
Mr. Wilhelm P. Sohnges, Germany
Dr. George Spaeth, Pennsylvania
Ms. Peggy Drewett String, Pennsylvania
Dr. Sy Trager, Washington, D.C.
Dr. Rita Ng Tseng, Hong Kong
Dr. L. Turkish, Louisiana
Ms. Colleen Roe Voras, Indiana
Dr. Harry Wachs, Pennsylvania
Mr. Ivan Wainer, England
Dr. Norman Wallis, Pennsylvania
Dr. Newton Wesley, Illinois
Dr. Paul White, Massachusetts
Dr. Otto Wichterle, Czechoslovakia
Dr. Edward Williams, Colorado
Mr. & Mrs. George Wodak, Israel
Mrs. DeDe Woolf, Pennsylvania.

I'D ALSO LIKE TO THANK THE MANY STUDENTS OF OPTOMETRY, THE residents in ophthalmology, and all the other fine people at the following outstanding institutions of higher learning: New York Medical College, Valhalla, New York; the Pennsylvania College of Optometry, Elkins Park, Pennsylvania; Albany Medical College, Albany, New York; Pennsylvania State University College of Medicine, Hershey, Pennsylvania.

The list is long but surely incomplete. When you know very little, have a lot to learn, and love to learn it—it makes one not want to miss the chance to say thanks.